Scottish Offpiste Skiing &
Nevis Range and Ben Nevis

A Guide to Skiing & Snowboarding Offpiste, Steep Skiing, ar

by Kenny Biggin

Photos & Diagrams by Kenny Biggin except where otherwise stated.

Entry diagrams by Ali Martin: www.westcoastart.co.uk

Design and layout by lamontdesign: www.lamontdesign.co.uk

SkiMountain logo design by www.crofteleven.co.uk

Cover Images:

Front: Hidden Gully. Photo: John Sutherland, Rider: Kenny Biggin

Back top: Powder in Bold Rush.

Back left: Back Corries. Rider: John Sutherland

Back middle: Bhealaich Face. Rider: Neil Muir

Back right: Don't Rush. Rider: Donald Paterson

1st Edition by Kenny Biggin 2013

Published by SkiMountain

SkiMountain Ltd

www.SkiMountain.co.uk

f /SkiMountain.co.uk

ISBN 978-0-9926065-0-3
A catalogue record of this book is available from the British Library

Acknowledgements

Big thanks go to Ali Martin for doing the entry diagrams and for all the support and encouragement (and for humouring me), all my skiing buddies, and everyone who has shared photos and information about routes and conditions. Huge thanks to Spike, Sudsy, Ian Milton and the other guys who made Nevis Range happen, and of course my parents for getting me into skiing in the first place.

Thanks also to the following: Nevis Range and SAIS staff, Dave Biggin, John Sutherland, Neil Muir, Donald Paterson, Blair Fyffe, Scott Muir, Martin Burrows-Smith, Seb Rider, Graham Moss, Mark Hughes, Frazer Coupland, Mick Tighe, John Wrighton, Dave Taylor, Davie Austin, Steve Wilcox, Ben Thorburn, Gav MacKay, Stevie McKenna, Doug Bryce, Spike Sellers, Simon Christie, Blair Aitken, Peter MacKenzie, Gavin Caruthers, Andy Nelson, Dave & Claire MacLeod, Ron Cameron, Jeff Starkey, Al Reid, Alan Kimber, Roger Wild, Marian Austin, Dougie Pryce, Mark & Niki Trigg, Gavin Miller, Heather Negus, Neil Fleming, Gus MacLellan, Nick March, Jakub Simon, Dave Parfitt, Brian Morrison, Kieran Hughes, Al Todd, Liam Moynihan, Bob Hyde, Charné Hawkes, Michael Yule, Mike Jardine, Gordon Fraser, Andy Burton, Bridget Thomas, Swampy Dave Roberts, Billy Lamont, Joe Barnes, Chris MacPherson and Jimmy Ness. Apologies to those I've missed out. Thanks also to all our sponsors.

Disclaimer

Offpiste skiing and boarding are inherently dangerous activities in an unpredictable environment. Routes can and do change dramatically depending on conditions. You must decide for yourself what you are and aren't capable of doing, and whether the conditions are favourable at any particular time. It is good practice to build a margin for error into your activities and allow for 'what-if' scenarios such as equipment failure, inaccurate information, avalanches, falls, and other dangers. You must also be aware of the impact your decisions can have on other mountain users and the dangers that you expose them to.

Forward

Writing this book has been a dream of mine for a long time - starting from skiing 'over the back' at Nevis Range every chance I got as a kid back in the early nineties. It has taken a long time to accumulate enough quality offpiste and ski mountaineering days in these hills to be able to do this book justice but hopefully I have finally done it.

There will probably always be 'one more line to ski' to make the book comprehensive but those lines can wait for future editions and for other skiers – would you have it any other way?

I have tried to strike a good balance between showing you what is on offer without spoiling the adventure of the unknown – only time will tell whether I have got that right.

I hope you get as much enjoyment out of this book and the adventures that follow as I got out of writing it – it's been a blast! Thanks for the good times to everyone I've skied these lines with over the years, and to those who got scared along the way, myself included, there's always next year. Here's to lots of snowy winters!!

Kenny Biggin, Spean Bridge, October 2013

We'll post any updates and new routes to you if you:
Like us on Facebook – /SkiMountain.co.uk

or:

Register your book – info@skimountain.co.uk
(subject: 'registerNR + name', no other text required)

Contents

photo **Kenny Biggin**

Introduction

This is a guidebook aimed at showing you the amazing skiing and boarding on offer in the Nevis Range and Ben Nevis area near Fort William.

Nevis Range offers the biggest lift-accessed offpiste freeride skiing area in Scotland, while Ben Nevis is the highest mountain in Britain and its famous North Face provides the greatest concentration of classic steep and long offpiste descents in the country.

The book not only provides route by route descriptions with as many good colour photos and illustrations as could be crammed in, but also includes chapters on the history, equipment, safety, tactics, knowledge and techniques required to get the most out of skiing and boarding in these mountains.

Every route included in this book has been skied at least once – the vast majority of them have been skied by the author and for the few that haven't, as close to a first hand account of the route as possible has been used. There are a handful of harder routes included that have seen attempts but descents so far have been incomplete, this is stated clearly in the text. There are of course a few lines that will 'go' that have yet to be skied by the author or anyone else as far as is known – that's not to say they have not been skied, but these have not been included in this book!

Although the guidebook is centred around Ben Nevis and Nevis Range, it also covers a selection of routes on the adjacent mountains – Carn Mor Dearg, Aonach Beag, and The Grey Corries, along with a small selection of local ski tours.

Although written by a skier, this book is aimed at all forms of snowsports including skiing, telemarking, snowboarding, and any others. Instead of trying to be politically correct the whole way through, the terms 'ski', 'skier' and 'skiing' have often been used generically to cover whatever the reader's chosen sport is. Please don't take offence to this as it makes the book much more readable than having to say 'skiers or boarders' every time.

Sharing

The decision to share the location of these routes has not been taken lightly - will this book condemn secret powder stashes to being tracked out straight away? Will currently remote and peaceful bowls become full of freeriders and less wild? Some of this evolution began with the construction of the lifts in 1989; and then later the construction of the Braveheart lift further opened the Back Corries up to the masses. There is a big enough selection of routes and few enough Scottish skiers that it's hard to see that overcrowding will become a problem here… and if it did, perhaps it would pay for more lifts!

Some local riders no doubt would prefer to keep the Back Corries to themselves, but it is hoped that one or two guidebook-informed runs down such classics as Bold Rush on the West Face, or the Rough Couloir on Aonach Beag (which they might not otherwise have done) will be enough to change their minds.

In writing this guidebook it is hoped that more people will be encouraged to enjoy and explore the amazing skiing offered by this area – in part because Nevis Range needs people to continue to ski here so that the operation remains sustainable. This guidebook provides almost a hundred different alternatives so there should be plenty of room for everyone.

Route Descriptions and Grading

Skiing and boarding offpiste is by its nature a free and non-prescriptive activity and this fact has tried to be reflected when writing this guide. Although the descriptions are based around each different route, there are often many variations and the difficulty of a particular line can vary enormously depending what the conditions are like at the time.

Illustrated Panel

similar to:	Easy Gully
harder than:	Rush
combine with:	Carn Mor Dearg

An illustrated panel is provided to give you an overall impression of each route which should allow you to make your own judgement calls about what you are ready to tackle and when. Comparisons are often made with other routes you may have skied already so that you can gradually work your way up and build an understanding of the routes which are appropriate for your ability as you go along. If you haven't skied much in this area before then you would be well advised to start off by skiing some of the easier sounding routes, or even the normal runs on the front of Nevis Range. Good first routes for anyone new to the back of Nevis Range are Yellow Belly, Backtrack or Winger Wall. Likewise, a good place to start skiing on Ben Nevis is an ascent of the normal Mountain Track followed by a ski down the Red Burn, or on a good day perhaps into Number 4 Gully or the Abseil Posts route in Corrie Leis.

Difficulty Rating

All of the runs in this guidebook are offpiste backcountry routes – they all travel through avalanche terrain and all of them (even the easiest) have hazards such as ice, rocks, or cruddy snow that can injure the unwary.

There hasn't been a tradition in Scotland of offpiste guidebooks or grading offpiste routes, so in writing this guidebook a decision had to be made about which, if any, existing system to adopt. Since the skiing in Scotland is uniquely... Scottish, and there are a variety of perceived problems with other grading systems from abroad, it seemed to make sense for a new grading system to be used. Most routes fall fairly easily into a small number of grades, so using 1 to 5 seems to work well.

The system often used in the Alps has grade subdivisions such as 3.2, 5.1, or 5.4. However, the system used here should not be confused with the Alpine one and has no subdivisions. This Scottish system assumes each difficulty rating covers a fairly wide spectrum and offers more of a strong hint about a particular route's difficulty rather than an extremely precise grading which is impossible in such an ever changing environment.

There are a few routes that have been skied (often only once) that even in rare conditions are only just skiable. Rather than leave the 1-5 system open ended which in other sports tends to encourage 'grade hunting', this book bundles anything falling beyond the fifth grade into a single category labelled simply 'X' which means 'not graded'.

The most important reason not to grade these marginal routes is to try to encourage people to ski them for the right reasons - ski them to test yourself, to commune with nature, to ski a dream line. Some things should be done for yourself and nobody else - would you still ski it if you knew nobody would ever know you'd skied it? Yes, at the 'X' level they are all hard, and some will be harder than others - but **which route is most difficult or most steep should become unimportant in comparison to the aesthetics of the line and its personal appeal to the skier. Take pride in your ability to complete runs successfully, safely, in good style, in making good decisions and never having dangerous epics.**

The Back Corries - Summit Corrie and Corrie an Lochain

Scottish Offpiste Route Grades

Author's Note: All grades assume good conditions

1 These routes are the most accessible offpiste runs and **in nice snow** will be options even for intermediate skiers. There will not be any significant steepness to contend with and the runs will rarely be steeper than a red run. In some cases these routes will be accessed via a harder route or some ski touring.

- **Adrenaline Scale:** Fun and Not Steep
- **Example Routes:** Gondola Line, Braveheart Chair

2 These routes start to provide an introduction to steeper offpiste skiing. The routes will largely be similar to black runs, but will often be steeper than this at the start. The routes will be open in nature and **in good conditions** falls will usually not be serious.

- **Adrenaline Scale:** Not too Steep
- **Example Routes:** Backtrack, Yellow Belly, Winger Wall

3 The skill level required for these routes begins to go up with short sections (usually at the entrance) starting to be quite steep.

- **Adrenaline Scale:** Quite Steep
- **Example Routes:** Chancers

4 These routes involve significant steepness and often take place in well defined gullies rather than open bowls. Some (not all) of these routes will be steep enough to be described as a Grade I winter climb in the climbing guidebooks.

- **Adrenaline Scale:** Very Steep
- **Example Routes:** Easy Gully

5 These routes are very serious and will involve very steep, sustained, and sometimes exposed skiing. Only the most solid of skiers should try these routes as falls are likely to be punished severely. These routes will all be steep enough to be described as Grade I winter climbs in the climbing guidebooks, and some (not all) may have sections steep enough to be classed as Grade II. Some of these routes may require ropework and mountaineering skills to complete safely.

- **Adrenaline Scale:** Extremely Steep
- **Example Routes:** Hidden Gully, Number 2 Gully, Don't Rush

X These routes are generally extremely tenuous and will hardly ever get skied. They become more like psychological challenges and tend to be undertaken during exceptional conditions by those with a need to test themselves. Often these routes will be classed as Grade II or even Grade III winter climbs.

- **Adrenaline Scale:** Good Luck
- **Example Routes:** Raeburn's Easy Route, Forgotten Twin, The Solar Face

The variation brought by snow conditions can't be stressed strongly enough – for example a level 4 route on a sheet ice day will often be far more treacherous than a level 5 route on a spring snow day. In addition, remember that some of these routes will only have been done a small number of times (perhaps only once) and possibly in very uncommon conditions – the grade is an indication only and you should always exercise your own judgement, expect the unexpected, and leave yourself plenty of safety margin.

Comparisons

Advice will sometimes be given to show other routes which are either similar in difficulty (or character), or harder. Along with the route's description this should help you better understand the difficulty rating for a particular route.

Combinations

Some routes are great when combined with other routes. Any combination suggestions are entirely optional.

Aspect / Slope Direction

The slope aspect is the direction it faces – so a gully with a Westerly aspect faces towards the West. When reading the avalanche forecast take careful note of the aspects (and heights) that they say will be most dangerous and choose routes accordingly. Each route description has an aspect icon that shows you roughly which direction a route faces in – this should make it easy to compare with the hazard 'compass rose' image displayed on the avalanche report.

Icons

Quality – the SkiMountain logo has been used to indicate a very subjective quality rating by the author. Three logos shows that this is a real favourite - a 'must do' route, while none shows a distinct lack of affection for the route!

Axe – You should have an axe and probably lightweight crampons with you to do this route. You may need them to get to the top of the route, or on the descent itself.

Skins – This icon indicates that you will find doing this route easier if you have skins and a touring setup. They are never essential, but may well make getting to or from the route easier.

Rope – This icon shows that you should seriously consider taking a rope and associated mountaineering equipment with you for this route. The description will tell you whether there are compulsory abseils involved – sometimes you will be able to make the descent without needing the rope but carrying it just in case may be a sensible precaution. Of course one person's abseil is another's cliff hucking opportunity, so use your own judgement after reading the description to decide what equipment you need.

Note about Slope Angles

Many skiers put a lot of emphasis on the angle of a slope but this can change quite dramatically depending on snow build-up and also vary significantly through the length of the run. Even with an OS map and a magnifying glass, phone apps, inclinometers, or poles it is difficult to measure slope angles accurately and consistently so it can be quite a misleading way to describe a route. The difficulty of a route is always closely related to how steep it is, but also to its length, narrowness, how exposed it is, and how sustained it is. The combination of the grade, the description, and the comparisons with other routes should give you a better idea of how a particular run compares with others you have already done – ultimately that seems more useful than an angle.

Maps

All of the routes in this book are located well within the 1:50,000 Ordnance Survey Landranger Ben Nevis (Fort William & Glencoe) map, Sheet 41. For anyone at all serious about doing much skiing in this area it is worth getting this map, carrying a compass (and possibly a GPS and/or altimeter) and knowing how to use it all.

You may prefer to use a 1:25,000 map in which case the right one is OS Explorer 392 Ben Nevis & Fort William which also covers most routes in this guidebook including the Grey Corries. There is also a Harveys 1:25,000 map of the area and for those who like detail there is also a Harveys 1:12,500 map of the summit area of Ben Nevis.

A good tip is to cut out (generously) the section of map you think you need, mark the grid square numbers on, and laminate it – this is far easier to carry in the top of your rucksack with a compass so you are more likely to have it the odd time you get caught out and suddenly find you need it.

photo **Kenny Biggin**

Don't get lost!

The Lochaber Mountain Rescue Team also produce a laminated map card (available in local shops) showing the key navigation required to get off the top of Ben Nevis without falling down either the North Face or the notorious Five Finger Gully. There is also a free Mountaineering Council of Scotland leaflet *Navigation on Ben Nevis* available locally to help keep you right about the tricky navigation required.

It is easy to get caught out in a whiteout or severe clag on top of these hills – both Aonach Mor and Ben Nevis in particular have large flat plateaus on their summits surrounded by cliffs. Getting lost here is not a nice experience and the cliffs and cornices make it all the more dangerous. The key is to train yourself up and then try not to get lost in the first place!

Compass Interference

Be aware that many common objects can affect the reading of a compass – try waving your compass in front of your mobile phone, transceiver, or GPS and you will probably see the needle give the wrong reading. When you are using a compass make sure you hold it well away from any objects that will affect its reading. You should also be aware that prolonged proximity to such objects can semi-permanently knock your compass needle off-course, so store it somewhere sensible and be careful which bits of kit you put in the same pockets when on the hill.

Entry Diagrams

COIRE DUBH

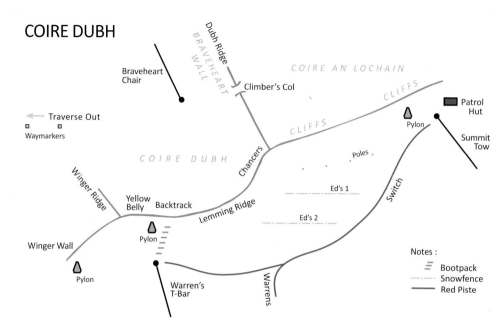

Each of the main sections of the book includes at least one entry diagram showing you where the start of the route is. They have been oriented to face in the direction you are most likely to arrive at the routes from. Some of the routes have GPS coordinates marked on them to help you find the right place and give you a bit more confidence about what you're dropping in to. Please note these are illustrations only and are not a substitute for maps, map reading, and common sense!

Weather and Snow Conditions

The North Face of Ben Nevis is perfectly capable of holding small amounts of snow year round. In some years the last remnants of snow have disappeared for a month or two but at the time of writing there has been snow there year round since 2006. Having said that it is still entirely reasonable to anticipate skiing possibilities as early as October and as late as June, though November to May is probably more realistic for all but the most enthusiastic.

photo **Mark Trigg**

Two foot of Pow!

Although seasons vary, the first dustings of snow tend to come in late September. The first skiable dumps usually come during October, November or early December – often during the Gondola's annual maintenance shutdown: just when your legs are at their pre-season weakest, you have to walk the furthest to get first tracks. Nevis Range will usually try to open at weekends if there is enough snow. Snow falling during October and November usually only lasts a few days before melting and there is rarely enough for a good base to develop. December and January frequently bring wild and windy weather in amongst further dumps of snow and / or rain, and every season these months bring intense speculation about whether it will be a good winter or not. If you time it just right or get lucky there can be some nice powder on offer during these early winter months.

February and March usually bring the most reliable ski conditions as by this time at least some sort of base has built up. April can be a great time for Scottish skiing, with longer and warmer days combined with spring snow. Most lifts usually close shortly after Easter because people stop turning up and buying tickets - but the Gondola stays open and this time of year can bring fantastic touring conditions with the North and Eastern slopes often holding plenty of snow well through May if not June.

Since it is warmed by the infamous Gulf Stream and North Atlantic Drift, this part of Scotland is very much warmer than other places sitting at 57° North. Despite this, the top of Ben Nevis has an average annual temperature of only just above freezing. There are frequent downpours of rain, and hurricane force winds are not unknown – as witnessed when the roof of the CIC Hut blew off and all but disappeared during the December 2011 gales.

The mountains can be clagged in with cold and wet for weeks (some would say months) at a time and Fort William locals tend to start most conversations by commenting on either the dreich weather or the midges. Having said that, when the clouds clear and the sun comes out the scenery is some of the best in the world and perhaps becomes all the more rewarding because of the preceding hardship.

The snow follows a similar pattern of reward and disappointment in Scotland – with frequent snowfalls invariably followed by melts or downpours (or both). Indeed the good snow years tend to be defined not so much by getting more snow as by having less thaws.

The prevailing wind comes from the South West as low pressure systems spin out of the Atlantic and across the North of Scotland. This weather pattern is most common and tends to load snow over the back of Nevis Range and Ben Nevis, building huge cornices and filling up the predominantly North and Easterly facing gullies and bowls.

Sometimes the jet stream gets bumped off its usual course which has the effect of allowing cold air to blow in from the Arctic and Siberia – when this happens Fort William gets hit with a generally Northerly or Easterly airflow bringing with it intense cold snaps known to take us down as low as minus twenty for short periods.

Web Resources

There are a variety of good resources to check weather conditions, snow conditions, and what others have been up to.

- SportScotland Avalanche Information Service: www.sais.gov.uk/page_lochaber.asp
- Met Office Mountain Weather Forecast: www.metoffice.gov.uk/loutdoor/mountainsafety (click on West Highlands)
- Mountain Weather Information Service: www.mwis.org.uk/wh.php
- Nevis Range - www.nevisrange.co.uk
- SkiMountain - www.SkiMountain.co.uk

Facebook pages and groups:

- /SkiMountain.co.uk
- /NevisRangeSNOW
- /BackCorries
- British Backcountry group

It is also well worth keeping an eye on the various ski forums and other ski information sites as well as what the climbers are saying – there are a number of local mountaineering guides and instructors who regularly post conditions updates, avalanche reports etc. which can give you valuable additional information to help your decision making.

An avalanche in Chancers narrowly missing the top of Braveheart Chair

photo Graham Moss / SAIS

Avalanches, Tactics & Safety

Despite the fact that Scotland doesn't get quite as much snow as places like BC, Alaska, the Alps, or Japan, we still have our fair share of avalanches. During the 2013 season there were eight deaths in Scotland due to avalanches, one of whom was an offpiste skier. Generally when we get snow it arrives with wind, which has the positive effect of filling up the bowls and gullies, but the adverse effect of creating wind slab. Frequent wind-loading combined with the regular shifts in temperature have a habit of creating unstable conditions which all offpiste skiers and boarders should be constantly aware of and prepared for.

The SportScotland Avalanche Information Service (SAIS) provide avalanche forecasts throughout the winter months (usually from around the end of December through to mid April) which can be accessed in a number of places including their website www.sais.gov. uk. The avalanche forecast is also posted on the Back Corries information board at the Nevis Range top Gondola station, along with useful updates and conditions observations from ski patrol. This board also has weather information

photo **Graham Moss / SAIS**

A small 10cm deep slab in Easy Gully – easily big enough to flush you down a chute / over cliffs etc.

and a transceiver check station so stopping at this board on your way past each day is a good habit to get into.

Reading the SAIS avalanche forecast the evening (or morning) before going skiing offpiste should become second nature. It tells you what the conditions were like when they were assessed, what the weather has done and will do, and it predicts what the conditions are likely to be like tomorrow. Forecasting avalanches is an inexact science and as with weather forecasts, it is just that – a forecast. It is important to emphasise that the avalanche forecast will never tell you what the avalanche hazard IS – only what it WAS and what it is LIKELY TO BE in the future.

The SAIS Forecasts are based on thorough on the hill observations and a detailed, purpose produced weather forecast so they have a great track record of being correct and are the best starting point for your risk assessment. Once in a while the weather forecast will be slightly off (for instance stronger winds, more precipitation, warmer temperatures, or a different wind direction) and in those circumstances the avalanche forecast may also be slightly out - so they should be treated as a crucial part of your risk-assessment process but not as an excuse to stop thinking and taking responsibility for yourself. Most importantly, when you get to the top of a slope you must reassess the avalanche hazard and associated risks yourself using all the information at your disposal.

The avalanche hazard scale has five levels - Low, Moderate, Considerable, High, and Very High. It's well worth studying the descriptive advice text used in the latest version of the hazard table on the www.sais.gov.uk website. Do not make the all too common skier's mistake of mentally downgrading a 'Considerable' avalanche forecast to 'Safe' - there is a CONSIDERABLE avalanche hazard on these days!

The Grey Zone

Unfortunately making a decision about whether a slope is safe to ski or not is an extremely tricky task, and one that even people with years of experience and training sometimes can get wrong. This is primarily a guidebook rather than a book about avalanches, so you should think seriously about going on a dedicated avalanche awareness course and / or reading some of the many good books about the subject. The following section is far from comprehensive but attempts to give you a quick overview of some of the main avalanche awareness issues and provides some introductory advice about how to ski safely.

If you want to be relatively safe from avalanches, stick to gentle slopes (with nothing steep above them) of under 30 degrees. As a rough guide, slopes similar in steepness to the lower half of the Goose are very unlikely to slide, whereas slopes steeper than the top of the Goose gully should be considered potentially avalanche prone. Avalanches are most common on the angles of slopes that are best for offpiste skiing (i.e. 35 to 45 degrees), particularly in the 24hours following heavy snowfall, rain, or significant wind-loading. Avalanches also happen on steeper slopes (50 degrees and over) but as the slope gets steeper the snow tends to sluff off more readily stopping it build up so much – however, a tiny sluff (or cornice collapse) in a steep and exposed gully can be enough to send you over cliffs etc, so steeper generally means more danger even though large slab avalanches become less common.

Because it is usually the time when large numbers of offpiste skiers and dangerous conditions intersect the most, the majority of fatalities happen on days with a 'Considerable' hazard forecasted (though there are still plenty on other days). Invariably if you are skiing offpiste in Scotland you will be skiing in 'The Grey Zone' – where you can't say a slope is completely stable, but nor are you likely to say it's death on a stick – avalanche avoidance would be a piece of cake otherwise!

Lines of Defence

You should look at avalanches as your enemy – they are out to get you... So you should do everything you can to defend yourself. There are a number of lines of defence that you can employ in your fight for survival, and you should use them all. The more heavily you rely on the inner circles of defence, the more likely you are to come a cropper! If you can't tick any of the boxes in the Avoidance, Protection, or Retrieval circles of defence then you are relying entirely on Luck – everybody has a little bit of Luck, but you can't do anything to influence it so you have to ask youself

❝ Do you feel lucky?... **Well do you?**

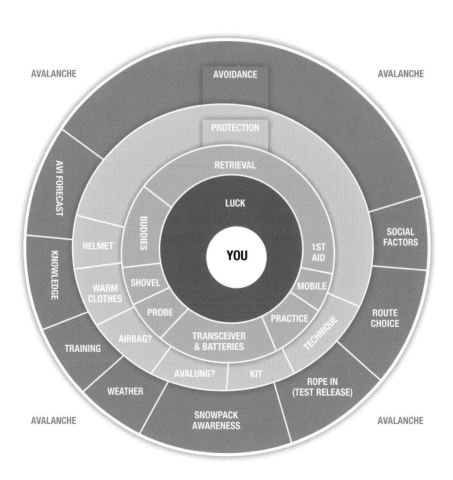

Assessing the Risk

So, how do you go about making a good decision?

Some things to think about:

- Don't ski avi prone slopes (i.e. anything steeper than the Goose) 24hrs after heavy snowfall or rain.
- Don't ski on heavily wind loaded slopes.
- Beware if the temperature is rising significantly.
- Get cautious if there has been a prolonged cold snap (as this is when 'faceting' occurs which creates a weak layer in the snowpack). Cold weather also tends to prolong instabilities after snowfall or wind loading.
- Don't ski un-survivable terrain (i.e. slopes on which a slide would put you over cliffs, into terrain trap gullies, etc).

Of course sticking rigidly to this is tricky so a pragmatic approach is required whereby you start the day with a clear idea about the forecast hazard, what the weather has done, and which routes might be a good idea. Then constantly gather information on the hill and risk assess slopes, so that you can make decisions about what is and isn't a good idea to ski.

One way to do a little risk assessment for yourself is to imagine a skewer (or a ski pole) sticking out of the ground with nothing on it; then create a mental image of a doughnut for each of the danger signs you think is applicable to skiing the particular route; now throw each of these doughnuts onto the skewer. The doughnuts can change in size depending on their perceived significance and only experience will tell you how big to make each doughnut on a particular day. The higher the stack on the pole, the greater the risk. Only you can decide how much risk is too much, but if you're looking at a high stack of doughnuts – take care, you may be biting off more than you can chew!

- High Avi Forecast
- Recent Avi Activity
- Strong Winds
- Shooting Cracks and Blocking
- Whumping Noises
- Subsidence (Cracks)
- Slopes over 30 degrees
- Convexities
- Bad Visibility
- Slow Group
- No Safety Kit
- No Transceiver Practice
- Terrain Traps
- Cliffs
- No Island of Safety

- Skiing Alone
- Large Group
- Little Frequented Route
- Aspect Matches Avi Report
- Altitude Matches Avi Report
- Rapid Temperature Rise
- Buried Weak layers
- Slabby Snow
- Good Sliding Surface Beneath
- Recent Rain
- No Helmets
- Unstable Cornices
- Prolonged Cold
- 6th Sense Saying No

Recent Deep Snow

INCREASING RISK

Although your instinct and sixth sense is probably not very accurate, you should still listen to your gut when it's sending you danger signals – if you feel like it's the wrong day, it probably is. The more experience you gain, the more 'tuned-in' your instinctual avalanche radar will become. Walking away when things don't feel right is ALWAYS the right decision – better to live to ski another day when you feel less twitchy about conditions.

Approaching from Above

For the majority of routes at Nevis Range this is the most likely scenario: you have come straight up the lifts, possibly had a run on the Goose, then you've traversed across from the Summit Tow to the top of a route you plan to ski. What do you do now?

   ❝❝ What do you think?

   ❝❝ It **looks** fine – I'll do it if you do!

Huck & Hope

You and all your buddies slide straight to the edge, have a quick glance, smack the lip with your poles, then huck off the cornice all at the same time and hope for the best. Many people have got away with precisely this approach for years at Nevis Range, but it's asking for trouble and is a ticking time bomb waiting to go off.

Before you go Anywhere:

- Check the avalanche report.
- Note what the weather has been doing and establish whether it has done what the avalanche forecasters thought it was going to or not.
- Before leaving the house get a good idea in your head of the aspects and routes that should be considered 'no-go', and some others that are safer alternatives.
- Don't ski alone.
- Speak to ski patrol and read information boards.
- Make sure you and everyone you're with has avalanche transceiver, shovel, and probe and the ability to use them.
- Do a transceiver check to make sure everyone is 'turned on'.
- Mobile phones are also a very important piece of safety kit – make sure yours is fully charged before going up.
- Look and listen for warning signs on your way up the hill – has there been lots of snow (or rain) recently, has the wind been loading your slope overnight (have new cornices formed, has the wind scoured one slope and loaded another), is a significant temperature change in progress, has there been a prolonged cold snap? Can you see other recent avalanche activity? Are there any classic bad signs such as cracks in the snow, blocks breaking off, whumping sounds, shooting cracks as you ski? Could you ski a safer slope first?

photo **Steven McKenna / Nevis Range**

Getting to the Edge

The first thing you need to contend with is the cornice and finding a way to the edge. The cornices at Nevis Range (and elsewhere) can be huge, and when a big one collapses it can crack a surprisingly long way back from the actual edge and take large sections of snow from all around with it. As soon as you go beyond where you can see rocks under your feet you are potentially standing on a cornice.

Depending on where the wind has been blowing from there is usually an aspect or one edge of a gully that is less corniced than elsewhere. By taking your time and walking or skiing up or down the ridge a little you can usually find a safe place from where you can get a better view of a section of the ridge that has less of a cornice. Leave your buddy at this vantage point so that they can direct you to the least overhanging part of the edge. If you have chosen wisely you are likely to be able to knock any remaining bits of cornice off with your pole. Sometimes you may even want to use your shovel or ice axe to carve out a bit of an entrance for yourself (but please don't ruin other people's fun by being over-zealous with knocking cornices off everywhere!). If it is too misty to see properly and you're not sure quite where to go then you either need to get a rope out or leave it for another day.

Assessing from Above

Having found your way safely to the edge, you now need to assess whether the slope below you is safe. Can you do this adequately by looking from above? Not really, no… so be careful!

The ideal when approaching from above is to find a small test slope which can give you an idea what the conditions might be like on the main slope. To be any use the test slope needs to be on a similar aspect (i.e. facing the same direction), and in a safe place. Be afraid, very afraid, of cracks shooting out from under your skis or blocks breaking away. Hollow 'whumping' sounds are also a big danger signal to listen out for.

There are only a few things you can do from above:

- Look for telltale signs – is there lots of wind loaded snow / are there recent sluffs or signs of debris elsewhere in the corrie / has it already slid / have other slopes on similar aspects been skied recently and if so do the tracks show any signs of instabilities?
- Break a bit of cornice off to see if it triggers a slide.
- By all means let someone else go first, but remember many avalanches release after the slope has been skied several times safely.

Before you start breaking large bits of cornice off or try to trigger avalanches, make sure you have established whether anyone is already in the corrie below you (for example climbers who've walked in from elsewhere).

If you decide you're going to ski it from above you need to recognise the risk you're taking and try to lower your chances of being caught:

- Be quick.
- Aim for a safe haven.
- 'Cut' the slope in one fast smooth traverse to a safe haven (but note people sometimes get pulled into avalanches when cutting a slope).
- Ski it one at a time.

Ropes

The only safe(ish) way to get to the edge and actually test the conditions is by using a rope. Even with this there are no guarantees but a rope does help you make a more informed decision and do some cornice management in safety. There isn't room to talk in depth about rope techniques here but some common anchors to use when roping to the edge or over are: in-situ posts, cat winch towers, snow bollards, skis in trenches, buddy axe belays, sling around boulders, etc – which is best on a particular day depends on location and snow conditions.

Roping in these days is less about digging a pit and more about seeing if the slope releases or exhibits warning signs such as shooting cracks, whumping noises, blocks breaking off etc – its primary usefulness is as a 'try before you buy' technique. On an unstable day you might rope in and set the slide off that might have killed you if you had just skied in! If you feel the need to do this you should also ask yourself whether you already know that the slope is suspect, and a different route choice would be a safer option. Many times roping in will probably tell you one of three things:

- It's icy and is definitely not avi-prone (but nor is it going to be a good ski).
- You set off a huge avalanche and it's obviously death on a stick.
- (By far the most common): you establish that this slope is in 'The Grey Zone' and have to make a judgement call accordingly. See the section about assessing The Grey Zone for more on this. (Yes, this is a circular section which gives no definitive answer to how to make the right decision – unfortunately that reflects the reality that there are no perfect answers!)

Going in for a closer look at The Solar Face (conclusion – not a good day for it!)   photo **Kenny Biggin** | rider **Donald Paterson**

Approaching from Below

For many routes, particularly on Ben Nevis, you are quite likely to be approaching your route from below. In this case you are facing different dangers to skiing from above – do you know how big and stable the cornice is at the top? Are there people above you? How stable are the slopes above you?

In some ways approaching from below is better in that you can regularly assess the snow pack as you go, look around you and spot other avalanche activity on similar aspects, and of course climbing a route prior to skiing it lets you see its difficulties first hand which can be particularly helpful on some of the steeper routes. Many people from a mountaineering background would always advocate approaching a steep ski descent by climbing it first.

However, you are inevitably travelling slowly going up and if you are there on the wrong day you are horribly exposed to danger from above or underfoot. To some extent you can mitigate the dangers during the approach by choosing your route carefully – for instance sticking to ridges and away from 'terrain traps'. But on somewhere like Ben Nevis if your plan is to climb up the gully you plan to ski, there comes a point where there is no choice but to either go home or expose yourself – this is a judgement call you'll have to make for yourself. All you can do to reduce the risks at this point is to leave big gaps between people and continually re-assess the danger signs, ideally turning back long before straying into the danger zone. If it is anything other than very stable, with minimal cornice hazards from above, then approaching in this way is a stressful option!

photo **Matt Groves** | rider **Al Bird**

Approaching Tower Gully by climbing it first

Approach from Below, then Above

A good compromise can be to approach your route in such a way that lets you get a good view of your route from afar while also giving you access to some small lower slopes on similar aspects allowing you to gauge the snow stability in something resembling safety. But then if it looks relatively safe, continue to the top by travelling up a much safer route (for instance up a rocky ridge). Then when you get to the top you can assess again from above (perhaps with the aid of a rope) and combine this assessment with the insights you gleaned lower down to inform your judgement calls about whether and what route to ski.

Debris covering the Mountain Track above the halfway lochan on Ben Nevis

Snowpack Awareness

Going on an avalanche course, reading the right books, and gaining lots of experience with the right friends will give you much more information and knowledge about assessing snow stability, but even without formal training it's well worth getting into the habit of frequently having a look at the snowpack. This can take the form of getting your shovel out and digging a big pit and formally assessing conditions, but it can also just be a quick exploration using your hands and poles to give you some quick feedback about what's under your feet.

A good way to ruin your day - avi debris at the bottom of Spikes

Be aware that a pit will only provide a small (but still useful) insight into the stability of a slope – tests have shown that pits a few metres apart can vary widely. Never base a 'GO' decision on the basis of a stable pit as it could easily be an isolated stable pocket on an otherwise very dangerous slope.

It's useful to get into the habit of doing quick test pits as you're skiing around – just use your hand or poles to isolate a block of snow about 30cm or a foot square and deep enough to go down to the last obviously stable layer (often ice here). Run your finger through the snow on the face of your block to get an idea of how hard or soft it is and whether there are different layers. Take note of whether the snow is sticking together in big slabs or is loose, and see if the block or parts of the block slide easily.

If nothing else, this will start to give you more awareness of what you're skiing on, how it varies over time and location, and how tricky it is to assess the danger!

Avalanche Equipment

If you intend to ski offpiste you should religiously wear a turned on transceiver and carry a small light rucksack with a shovel and probe in it. You should also pressure your buddies into doing the same. People often say they can't afford it ('maybe next year') but once you have bought these essential items of kit they will last for many years and not only might save your life, but might even allow you to save someone else's.

Once you own this kit, make a habit of using it every time you go skiing - irrespective of what the conditions are or what you think your plan is. Put your transceiver on when you put your salopettes on and turn it on at the same time (i.e. at breakfast). Do not turn it off until you are back home or in the pub. Replace the batteries regularly – as a matter of course at the start of each season and then keep an eye on the battery meter. Why not keep the battery percentage up above 90% - batteries are cheap. As important as owning and wearing this kit is knowing how to use it quickly and efficiently – take a course and make a point of practicing every season (if only to make sure your buddies will be able to find you quickly!)

Transceiver Check

Part of your daily offpiste skiing routine should become a transceiver check – an efficient way to do this is in two stages:

- **Stage 1:** Before you leave the carpark, do a transceiver check with your buddies (apart from anything else, this makes sure no-one has forgotten to put theirs on before you get further up the hill). Start off by standing some distance away from your group with your beacon on transmit while everyone else walks towards you on search (hopefully demonstrating they can find you). Everyone should now turn their beacons to transmit.
- **Stage 2:** Whoever is first off the Summit Tow, (or first to the top North Face car park on the Ben) heads off away from the group and turns their transceiver to receive, then the rest of the group ski slowly past you at intervals so that you can check they are transmitting and that your beacon can pick them up. Make sure you finish the process by turning your own beacon back to transmit.

This simple two stage process keeps hassle to a minimum while ensuring everyone is wearing a turned on fully functioning transceiver and has at least a basic understanding of how to use it.

Helmets

Make wearing a helmet a habit as well – this may well save your life before a transceiver will! Remember that the transceiver, shovel and probe combo is used in the worst case scenario of someone getting buried in an avalanche – far better to stop the avalanche getting you by Avoidance instead. And consider carefully how well Protected you are (helmet, warm clothes, airbag, avalung) as being able to be found is only any use to you if you are still alive.

Other Avi Equipment

There is a small selection of other avalanche safety equipment items which fit into the 'Protection' category and are aimed at improving your chances of survival should you get caught.

Airbags are integrated into rucksacks and aim to keep you on top of the debris. Avalungs aim to slow down the process of asphyxiation by increasing your ability to get oxygen out of the snowpack and by redirecting your carbon dioxide away from your face. In the Alps and North America, these items (especially airbags) are becoming more and more mainstream - the statistics about them remain in the early days and the debate continues to rage online. The most sensible thing to say about them is that in certain circumstances they may increase your chances of survival.

As with wearing a transceiver, wearing an airbag should not be seen as a reason to stop making good decisions about route choice – as shown in the Lines of Defence diagram, Avoidance is better than Protection. On a final note on avi equipment, in his guidebook to the Espace Killy, Didier Givois makes a good point that since the first victim to be found by avalanche rescue dogs is usually the one with a sausage in their pocket, on 'dangerous days' you may want to stop at a butcher's on the way to the ski hill!

Crown wall left by avalanche on walk out route from West Face

photo **Graham Moss / SAIS**

BEING
PREPARED

WITH OUR NEW
REMOVABLE AIRBAG SYSTEM

The **REMOVABLE AIRBAG SYSTEM** equips
you for critical situations – or saves weight
and gives you extra backpack volume.
VIDEO TUTORIAL and lots of knowledge on
ortovox.com

Finding your Buddies

If (despite all the great decisions you've made) the worst happens and you get avalanched, the most likely thing to save you (assuming you've worn your helmet, warm clothes, transceiver, zorbing suit etc) is speedy and efficient actions by your buddies. So make sure you ski with folk who carry transceiver, shovel, and probe and practise regularly with them so you know you are skiing with people who you can count on.

The most likely way for a person to survive burial is for their companions to dig them out fast. Do not waste valuable time going back to tell ski patrol or phoning for help at this point unless it can be done with a very quick shout or in parallel by other people. Your buddy's best chance is YOU.

As the avalanche happens try to keep your eyes on the victim for as long as possible, then as soon as the slope stops moving check it is safe to move yourself and go straight to the spot they were last seen. Tell the other skiers you're with to turn their transceivers to Search as well (most have an 'auto-revert' function to switch them back to transmit after a while in case of a secondary avalanche) and tell them to hang back but get their probes and shovels ready for use.

From the spot the victim was last seen get your transceiver out, switch to Search mode and begin a search. The exact technique varies depending which transceiver you have, and recommendations evolve over time. However, the basic process goes as follows.

Find Signal: Zig zag systematically down the avi path until you pick up an initial signal. Make sure you cover the entire slide path never leaving gaps of more than 15-20metres.

Follow Signal In: As soon as you pick up the signal, follow the signal in rapidly until you are within a few metres. Be quick but be careful not to go so fast that you muck this part up – it's all too easy on a steep slope to suddenly realise you've shot 20metres too low and wading back up will take ages.

Pinpoint: Take your skis off and hold your transceiver low right next to the snow in a cross shape to do a pinpoint search and mark the lowest reading with a pole. Accuracy here will save you time later.

Probe: Having found the lowest reading, whip your probe out and methodically probe around your marker in a gradually widening circular pattern until you find the body. Push your probe in perpendicular at right angles to the slope rather than vertically. Do not be tempted to skip the probing stage as it has been shown to dramatically reduce the time digging, even in a shallow burial. Leave your probe in place on the body and get your shovel out.

Dig: It has been shown that there is a real art to how to dig a victim out most efficiently, but in essence the best way is to dig in across the slope to them rather than down. If there are multiple helpers position them behind you to help clear the snow out of the way as you dig.

Clear Airway & Revive: As soon as you find the body, try to clear the face and airway as fast as possible. If required give them some rescue breaths and begin CPR to keep their blood pumping – make sure help is on its way pronto!

There are a variety of other techniques to learn and practise when it comes to searching for buried victims – for instance multiple burials, or if there are multiple searchers. These are best learnt on a course although there is also a transceiver park set up at the top of the Alpha Tow at Nevis Range where you can have a practice on a poor snow day or when your legs need a rest.

Getting Help

You should always try to be self sufficient and get yourself out of trouble if you can, but also recognise when you need help. If the worst should happen, stabilise the situation as much as you can and then contact any of the following (either yourself or via someone else) and give them as much information as possible.

Ski Patrol – can be contacted via radio by asking the lifty at the bottom of all tows. The patrol hut above the Summit Tow is also permanently manned. Even if you are outside the ski area boundary, if you have used the lifts to get up there contacting ski patrol is a good place to start – they will have this book and will have good knowledge about where you say you are and if necessary will be able to coordinate contacting external help from the police or mountain rescue if required.

Nevis Range – phone 01397 705825, then dial zero for the office. They have radio contact with ski patrol. Put this number in your phone now!

Police / Mountain Rescue Team – in an emergency contact the police directly by dialling 999. Tell them where you are, what's happened, and that you are likely to need the Mountain Rescue Team. If you are near the lifts make sure you tell them you're at Nevis Range, and if you can give them a grid reference, route name from this book, or GPS location even better. Even if it looks like you haven't got a mobile signal, you can sometimes still get through to 999. If you have registered your mobile in advance and find yourself unable to call, you can also send a text message to 999 – register your phone now simply by texting 'register' to 999 (more info at www.emergencysms.org.uk).

Lochaber Mountain Rescue Team (LMRT) is the busiest rescue team in the country and is entirely operated by volunteers. The team survives on donations and good will so use them as a last resort and support them any way you can – you can start by liking them on Facebook (search for Lochaber Mountain Rescue Team).

Nevis Range (Aonach Mor)

Back in 1970 two young climbers decided to try to make some much needed cash by gathering together all their own climbing gear, filling a small van with kit from suppliers, and sticking it up for sale in the window of a small rented shop by Fort William pier. Fifteen years later, Ian Sykes and Ian Sutherland had built up a successful outdoor retail business called Nevisport and were starting to think big! With the help of local hotel owner Ian Milton and after years of hard work, politics, and determination, they started to lay the first concrete foundations for a new Gondola system in the heart of Leanachan Forest. The newest ski resort in Scotland - Nevis Range - opened in 1989 and Fort William hasn't looked back since!

Author's Note: See the back of the book for more background and history.

photo **Jo Mackin** | rider **Dave Biggin**

Dialing in - Summit Tow terrain park

© SkiMountain

photo **Dougie Pryce**

Sunset from Nevis Range

photo **Kenny Biggin**
rider **Dave Biggin**

Great snow, bad vis - in the Goose

photo **Kenny Biggin**
rider **Mystery boarder**

Highlander Freestyle Series on the Summit Tow

photo **Kenny Biggin**
rider **Chris MacPherson**

Groomers keeping the pistes sweet

Snowboard Patrol on the early shift

photo **Kenny Biggin**
rider **'Swampy' Dave Roberts**

The Gondola takes six skiers at a time up to 650metres and from there eight lifts service the pistes on the front of the mountain while at the same time providing lift-access to the largest freeride skiing and boarding area in Scotland. Nevis Range has great skiing for all abilities, but where it comes into its own is the potential for good offpiste riders. Nevis Range tends to be heaps quieter than almost all of the other resorts yet sometimes has better and more snow – especially over the back.

The Front Side

Although this is a guidebook about offpiste, it makes sense to say at least a little about the front of the mountain – this is where (almost) all the lifts are and there can be some great skiing on offer here.

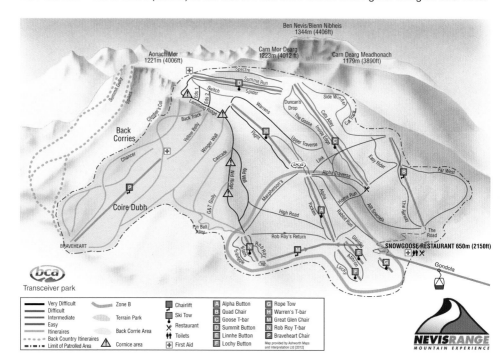

There are two main choices as you come out of the Gondola hall – go left and use the Linnhe beginner lift to get to the Alpha Button Tow, or go right and walk then ski along a track to the Quad Chairlift. In the mid-height section of the mountain there is the steep Warren's T-bar going on to the left from the top of Alpha, with the Goose T-bar to the right of the top of Alpha. Then from the top of the Goose there is the Summit Tow taking you up onto the summit plateau.

For serious skiers the combination of Alpha + Warrens, or Alpha + Goose + Summit tows are the arterial lifeblood of Nevis Range – they provide quick and good access to everything on the mountain so the staff try hard to keep them running smoothly! Boarders looking for comfort may want to go up the chair instead of Alpha to get to the Goose although this usually takes longer so won't be the powder hound's choice.

There is also the Great Glen Chair leading left from the Gondola which is primarily to take beginners across to the short but good Rob Roy T-bar.

Out of sight over the back there is the Braveheart Chairlift too, but more on that later.

© SkiMountain

There can be some great skiing on the front of the mountain but since this book is aimed at offpiste skiing we'll let you work out the rest about the front of the hill by yourselves.

Low Down

The days when you can ski to the top Gondola station can be few enough in some seasons. The days when you can ski all the way to the car park are extremely rare but once in a while it does happen – when it does, you have to ignore thoughts such as 'but these are my new skis' and just go for it!

There is actually some great skiing on offer in this section of the hill but even if there is lots of snow it's almost certainly going to be good at the top then pretty marginal lower down.

1. Gondola Line

The most obvious option for skiing to the car park is to ski down directly beneath the Gondola. This route leads you down around 250metres of good skiing until you get to the deer fence. From the fence the skiing will deteriorate pretty rapidly but the best bet is to follow the World Cup downhill mountain bike track which leads back to the car park. It will depend how much snow there is as to whether you want to follow the mountain bike track all the way down or opt for the mellower forest tracks – no matter how much snow there is you are likely to see sparks fly before getting to the bottom!

2. Allt an t-Sneachda

Start at the top of the Goose and go all the way down the gully line to the bottom of the chair – this can form a natural half-pipe feature and can be brilliant. If there is enough snow you can get a great ski by continuing down the gully below the chair. After a while head slightly left to join the Red mountain bike track as it heads through the deer fence into the forest. You can follow this path all the way down to the car park.

3. Sgurr Finnisg-aig

similar to:

harder than: Gondola Line

combine with:

When there's loads of snow you can take a long flat traverse out to skier's right from the Gondola top station. This takes you towards and then over a small ridge which gets you onto a steeper pitch coming down from Sgurr Finnisg-aig. You'll get around 200metres of great ripping before needing to head left to join the downhill mountain bike track that leads through the deer fence under the Gondola line. For the really adventurous why not walk up Sgurr Finnisg-aig and ski down from there. The skiing here is much steeper than directly under the Gondola line and has been skied only very rarely. Don't try skiing the far (North-East) side of Sgurr Finnisg-aig as there are cliffs and ice climbs here!

> ## "If there is a jewel in the crown of Scottish Skiing, it has to be the Back Corries of Nevis Range"

Nevis Range
... home of the back corries

Back Country [bak-cor-ees] n. **1.** :the off-piste Coire Dubh, Summit Corrie & Coire an Lochan **2.** :**Braveheart chair:** v. located in the Coire Dubh off-piste bowl to access Corrie Dubh and the extensive Back Corries area **3.** adj: **Nevis Range's** best kept secret . . .shh

back corrie workshops

transceiver parks

freeride clinics

nevisrange.co.uk   01397 705825

NEVIS RANGE
MOUNTAIN EXPERIENCE

The Back Corries

If there is a jewel in the crown of Scottish Skiing it has to be the Back Corries of Nevis Range – there are three big bowls with a great selection of different routes and all over a height of 900metres. There really is something for everyone in the Back Corries - on the right day intermediate skiers can slide their way into their first offpiste experience on Backtrack or Winger Wall, while skiers at the highest end of the ability spectrum can test themselves on some of the steepest lift accessed skiing in the world!

When Nevis Range first opened the Back Corries was strictly out-with the ski area boundary and as such it was up to the individual to make their own judgement calls about whether it was safe on that particular day or not. Some time after they built the Braveheart Chairlift the first bowl – Corrie Dubh – was brought into the ski area boundary as an 'off-piste bowl with named itineraires' and as such can now be one of three statuses: Open, Limited Patrol, or Closed.

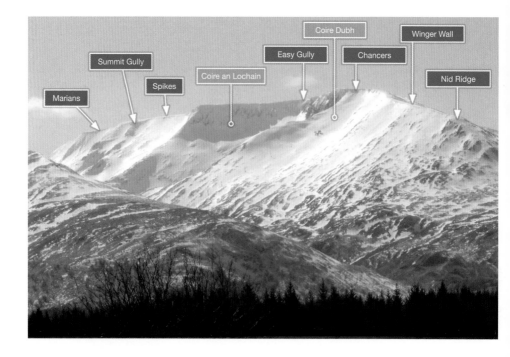

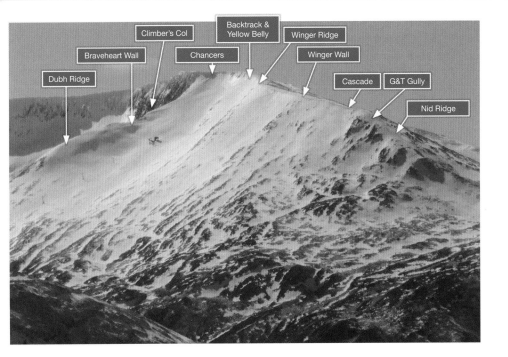

The Coire Dubh itineraries (including the Winger Wall to Nid area) will usually be designated as 'Limited Patrol', but may also at times be given an 'Open' or 'Closed' status. At the time of writing in 2013, Nevis Range's definition of the three statuses is as follows:

❝ **Limited Patrol** – 'The Coire Dubh itineraries are accessible for appropriately experienced and equipped skiers and boarders venturing off-piste. Limited Patrol activities include assessing conditions and posting notifications of hazards. Ski Patrol will assist anyone in difficulty or who has become injured however, being off-piste, this is likely to be complicated and time consuming. Ski Patrol will not normally sweep itineraries at the end of the day.'

❝ **Open** – 'The Coire Dubh itineraries are considered favourably accessible for advanced users, although still designated as off-piste. Patrol cover will be like the rest of the main ski area.'

❝ **Closed** – 'The Coire Dubh itineraries are considered unacceptably dangerous for any users. They are therefore out of bounds if being accessed by ticket holders. Tickets will be removed from any skier or snowboarder accessing the area when it is closed.'

All other areas of the Back Corries (i.e. Coire an Lochain and Summit Corrie) are designated as 'Backcountry' outwith the ski area boundary and are accessed after walking across the plateau. These other back country itineraries are not assessed by Ski Patrol although they will often have information about conditions etc.

photo **Mark Trigg**
rider **Niki Trigg**

This is an off piste area with challenging terrain.

Entry points are steep and snow conditons can vary

Check with ski patrol for up to date conditions.

Tread carefully & enjoy!

photo **Mark Trigg**

Happy days in the Back Corries

Wingers Area

When you arrive at the top of Warren's T-bar there is a traverse that leads off to the left hand side. If you follow this traverse it leads to an old cat-winching tower and just beyond the pylon lies the edge leading over the back at Winger Wall.

This section of the back corries is quite accessible and rarely all that steep, however big cornices can still form here, avalanches are possible, and a slide on ice here can be nasty. Provided conditions are good this is a brilliant area for relative newcomers to the offpiste experience.

Winching into Winger Wall

photo **Ian Sykes**

WINGERS & NID

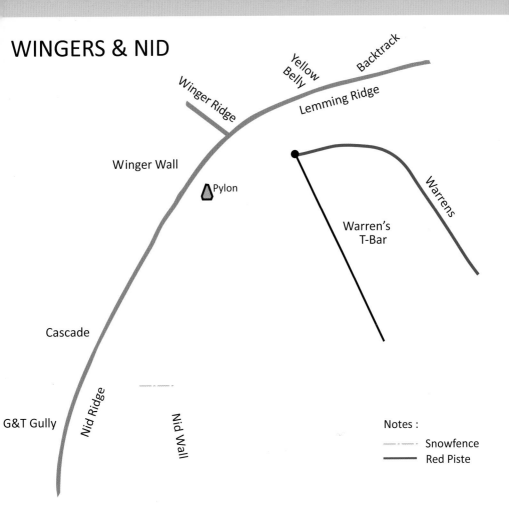

Winger Ridge

Yellow Belly

Backtrack

Lemming Ridge

Winger Wall

△ Pylon

Warren's T-Bar

Warrens

Cascade

Nid Ridge

Nid Wall

G&T Gully

Notes :

------- Snowfence

———— Red Piste

4. Winger Wall

similar to:	Backtrack
harder than:	
combine with:	

Having traversed out left from the top of Warrens you can access some great skiing by continuing over the edge. There is often a cornice here but if you look up and down the ridge a little you will find an entry point suitable for most appetites. If you look up to the right here you are looking up towards Lemming Ridge with Yellow Belly just out of sight. Winger Wall will usually have a short steeper section right at the top but then provides a nice open face leading down to where the traverse line from Corrie Dubh cuts across. On a good day there is loads of fun to be had by doing laps on Winger Wall using Warren's T-bar.

photo **Michael Yule**

Looking up Rob Roy T-bar to Nid Ridge

5. Nid Ridge

1-2

Nid Ridge is the long and well defined Eastern edge of the mountain that runs as an extension of Lemming Ridge all the way from the lower end of Coire Dubh down the East side of Aonach Mor. The run usually starts at the top of Winger Wall after coming up Warren's T-bar. You can stay on the edge of the ridge and glance to your right into the back all the way down. There can be some great opportunities for jumping back and forth over the ridge, especially lower down. In most snow conditions skiing down the ridge never gets too steep, though it can get quite icy when the wind has stripped it.

CHAM

Wanting to give freeriders and the all-mountain riders the best ski for their needs and dreams in this sector, Dynastar created the **Cham** collection. Flotation, manoeuverability, edge grip on pistes, stability in powder and amazing power out of the turn. And all wrapped up in a freeride ski that overcomes the usual face of convention. The new Cham's see it, ski it, love it!

Look higher
Go deeper !

DYNASTAR
Chamonix Mont-Blanc

Dynastar.com

photo **Kenny Biggin** | rider **Dave Biggin**

Airtime doing laps of Wingers area from Warrens

6. Cascade

similar to:	Winger Wall
harder than:	
combine with:	

As you ski along the ridge from the top of Winger Wall and look over the edge, you go over a slight plateau after a hundred metres or so which marks the start of the next snow slope along known as Cascade. This run is another that is great for relative offpiste novices and is very similar to Winger Wall. Cascade can be skied anywhere along to the next rock band and there are generally both easy ways in as well as good cornice jumping opportunities. The lines in this area can offer great skiing and provide a bit of variety if the back is getting skied out or you are ticking routes off!

7. G&T Gully

harder than: Winger Wall, Cascade

G&T Gully was skied by and named after the original Lochaber avalanche forecasters - Graham (G) Moss & Tom (T) Gilchrist. There is now often a route sign at the top of G&T - after Cascade, Nid Ridge begins to steepen and there are several distinct rocky ridges dropping off to the right with the main line being G&T Gully. The route is very similar in difficulty to Cascade and Wingers but has a more enclosed feel to it with rocky ribs on either side. This open gully provides more great skiing to drop into when you're doing laps of the back via Warren's T-bar.

8. Nid Wall

harder than: Nid Ridge

The Nid Wall is the steep and often rocky slope on the far left of Nevis Range as you look at it from the car park. In recent years it has suffered from a lack of snow build up, but when it's white enough it provides a great ski. It is on the piste map as a black run but it can be just as fierce as parts of the Back Corries and Ski Patrol will usually only open it when it's in 'good nic'. Access it by skiing down Nid Ridge from Warrens but when you sense the slope beginning to steepen after a couple of hundred metres, instead of continuing down the ridge you stay on the face. In good snow years there is snow all the way across between Nid Wall and the ridge making the distinction fairly blurred.

During the early nineties, the Nid Wall was also the location of The Flying K - a speed skiing course that started at the top of Nid Wall and went all the way across towards Sgurr Finnisg-aig.

Routes out from Wingers Area

All of the routes in the Wingers area lie directly above the traverse line that leads to skier's left back to the top of the Rob Roy T-bar. If you follow the fall line down from Winger Wall there are a series of permanent way-markers that you can link together to show you a good route out. The route takes you over a number of small slopes all of which can be known to avalanche so keep your wits about you. In risky conditions make sure you keep moving, travel across suspect slopes one at a time, and stop on the tops of ridges rather than in the terrain trap gullies.

Coire Dubh

When the majority of people talk about skiing 'over the back' this is the area they are talking about – it is a wide open bowl that now has the Braveheart Chairlift nestling within it. The Coire is a large semi-circle so the routes here are on a variety of different aspects which means snow conditions and stability can vary dramatically – the right hand side of Chancers is almost on a Northerly aspect, with most of the bowl being some variation of an Easterly aspect while the far end of Yellow Belly almost faces South.

Coire Dubh is best accessed from the Summit Tow though you can also bootpack directly up from the top of Warrens to get to Yellow Belly. If you are coming from the Summit Tow get off the top on the left – at this point there is likely to be information from Ski Patrol about what the current area status is and what entrances and snow conditions are like.

From the top of the Summit Tow you have three different route options (see entry diagram): the first is to skirt right along the edge of the cliffs next to the cornice – this option is for good confident skiers only as you need to stay well away from the huge cornices and obviously make sure you don't fall over the edge. The second route option is the most direct and takes you on a flat and often rock-strewn traverse straight across to the top of Chancers – there are often black poles marking this route at intervals but don't count on this if it's misty!

photo **Steven McKenna / Nevis Range**

Sweet lines in Chancers, Coire Dubh

The third route option is to follow the traverse lines Ed's1 and Ed's2 (named after local climbing legend Ed Grindley) – to access these, follow the traverse road leading from the top of the Summit Tow towards Warrens – you stay on the road until you pass the first small descent and turn, at which point you should break off the road to your right to follow either the first or second snowfence, both of which bring you out in between Chancers and Backtrack. All of these routes may well be icy and / or rocky so take care – there is almost always significantly more snow in the Back Corries than there will be on your way across to the edge.

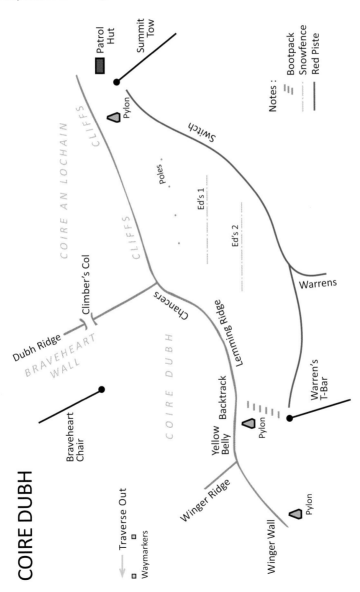

COIRE DUBH

photo **Jakub Simon** | rider **Mike Samler**

Switching it up near Backtrack with Lemming Ridge on the right

9. Lemming Ridge

similar to:		
harder than:		
combine with:	Nid Ridge, Warrens, Backtrack, Winger Wall

This is the route to take to get your first view into the Back Corries. Get to the top of Lemming Ridge by following the poles to Chancers or one of Ed's traverses. Without needing to be a good skier, and in good visibility when it's not icy, you can carefully follow the ridge all the way along and either choose to drop in down one of the routes described, or carry on down Nid Ridge, or even back out down onto Warrens.

If you don't like the look of the skiing off the edge into the bowl you can continue down the ridge with a view to skiing Nid Ridge or Winger Wall. If you really just want the psychological suffering to stop as soon as possible, the best plan is probably to turn your back on the steeps and ski away at right angles from the cornices - a hundred metres or so of gradual descent over the rocks should bring you back to the top of the main Warrens run at which point although still at the top of a steep piste, at least you are back on the front of the hill and can stick close to the snow fences if it's misty.

If you decide that the Coire Dubh bowl isn't for you, it is possible to continue down the ridge until you round the corner which divides Coire Dubh from Winger Wall. If you keep looking over to the right and don't fancy Winger Wall either, you can turn left when you reach a metal pylon which marks the way back towards Warrens.

Chancers in top nic, with Braveheart Chair below

photo Steven McKenna / Nevis Range

10. Chancers

3

similar to:	
harder than:	Yellow Belly
combine with:	Climber's Col, Braveheart Wall

Chancers is one of the classic 'over the back' lines at Nevis Range and probably the route most people have heard of. It is the name given to the very top of the Coire Dubh bowl and is steep enough to be ill-advised for newcomers to skiing over the back. There can be a large cornice with frequent windslab build up on the scarp slope at the top. You can either continue all the way down the fall line or head right towards the ridge line (Climber's Col) and traverse up onto Braveheart Wall.

This route was skied prior to the lifts being built but was named after some of the avalanche forecasters - The Chancers - who opted to drop into the steepest part of the bowl, while the Yellow Bellies took the easier lines to the skier's left.

Coire an Lochain looking sweet from Climber's Col

photo **Steven McKenna / Nevis Ra**

11. Climber's Col

similar to:	Braveheart Wall
harder than:	
combine with:	Backtrack, Chancers

After skiing the top of Chancers it is possible in some conditions to drop over the ridge to your right into Coire an Lochain. However, because of the aspect and prevailing weather this part of the hill is often fairly bare with lots of rocks. If it looks snowy and stable then there are some good adventures to be had here taking you down and round to the bottom of Braveheart. If the chair isn't running don't go all the way down – instead ski the first pitch and then break left through the rocks to a small plateau on the ridge from where you can do a pole push / skate traverse across to rejoin the main traverse line.

12. Backtrack

similar to:	Winger Wall
harder than:	
combine with:	Braveheart Chair

At various times Nevis Range have experimented with making the Back Corries accessible to the widest range of abilities – at points this has extended to cutting a groomer track into the side of the bowl to give people an easy traverse in past the main steep part at the top. Despite the fact that the groomer rarely cuts this traverse in these days, this route has become known as Backtrack and along with Winger Wall these are still usually the easiest ways into the Back Corries and the best options for people who want to have a shot on Braveheart but haven't the desire to scare themselves!

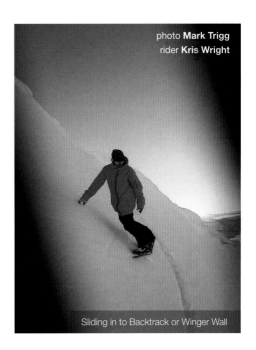

photo **Mark Trigg**
rider **Kris Wright**

Sliding in to Backtrack or Winger Wall

photo **Jakub Simon** | rider **Mike Samler**

13. Yellow Belly

similar to:	
harder than:	Backtrack
combine with:	

Yellow Belly has at times been used as the generic name for the majority of the Coire Dubh bowl apart from Chancers. Despite the fact that it probably got skied several years prior to the lifts being built, one of the early Nevis Range instructors, Frazer Coupland, has been dining out for over twenty years now on the fact that this route was named after him! Currently the piste map marks Yellow Belly as being a line to the left of Backtrack but this should not put you off going in wherever takes your fancy right around the bowl. It is primarily a case of finding a route that you like the look of. Cornices can form the full length of the bowl so people often look for the line of least resistance. The principle difference between Backtrack and Yellow Belly is whether you do a long traverse to get into the bowl (Backtrack), or ski more directly down the fall-line (Yellow Belly).

THE DUDES OF HAZZARD

Dave dropping the rocks to the left of Chancers

photo **The Dudes of Hazzard** | rider **Dave Biggin**

14. Main Bowl

2

similar to:

harder than: Yellow Belly

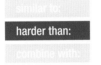

combine with:

Although not currently marked on the piste
map as itineraires, there are many different
skiable lines in the bowl in between Backtrack
and Chancers. Which line you choose to take
will depend on your taste for cornices, rocks,
steepness, etc. so keep an open mind and see
what you like the look of.

Looking round the main bowl of Coire
Dubh with Chancers at the top

photo Matt Groves

skimountain

15. Winger Ridge

similar to:	
harder than:	Winger Wall
combine with:	

When conditions in the back are icy this broad rocky ridge just to the left of Yellow Belly will usually soften first since it catches the sun from when it rises right through until it disappears behind the hill in the afternoon. There are also some great lines to be had weaving your way down between (or over!) the various rock bands here. There is a steep pitch right at the top of the ridge in between two rock bands which makes a great place to practise your jump turns.

16. Braveheart Chair

similar to:	The Goose
harder than:	
combine with:	Backtrack

The Braveheart Chair was won by Spike during a poker game in Siberia, from a group of Russian Cossack mafia who later took their revenge by coming to Scotland and cutting the footrest bars off. Such rumours about the Braveheart Chair abound but, whatever the actual history, it has been the subject of much discussion from Nevis Range locals. When running, the chair not only has some great skiing down beneath it, but also provides skiers with the means to regain the traverse line back to the restaurant.

To get to the Braveheart Chair you need to ski in from above via a slightly harder line – the easiest route in is Backtrack which on a good snow day is accessible to good intermediate skiers – once you have got past the initial steep part of that route, just aim for the top of the chair and then ski down roughly underneath it. The terrain here is actually really good fun and skiing this lift is a completely different experience to the front of the mountain so should be on everyone's hitlist.

As well as the great skiing to be had close underneath the Braveheart Chair, you can break out right and pick your way in amongst the rocky ribs. There are a couple of shallow gullies here named Kim's and Alison's after ski racer Kirsteen 'Kim' McGibbon and mountaineer Alison Hargreaves.

Author's Note: The true story is only slightly less amusing – Spike found the lift lying in a field in Passo Tonale in Italy and bought it for a fraction of its actual value. The footrests had to get cut off due to a miscalc when building the off-ramp!

Bluebird under the Braveheart Chair with Chancers above

photo **Mark Trigg** | rider **Niki Trigg**

BRAVEHEART
SECTOR

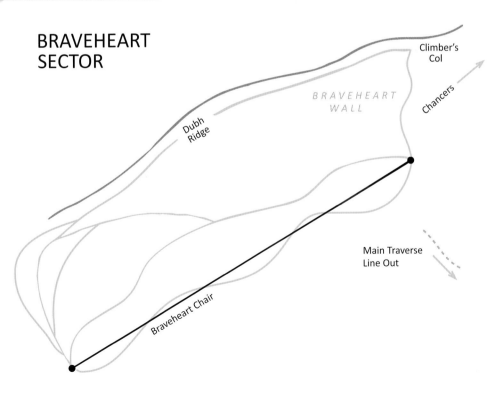

Climber's
Col

*BRAVEHEART
WALL*

Chancers

Dubh
Ridge

Main Traverse
Line Out

Braveheart Chair

17. Braveheart Wall

similar to:	
harder than:	Braveheart Chair
combine with:	Chancers

The short but sweet North / North-East facing slope above the top of the Braveheart Chair is a great way to finish skiing Chancers. Ski to the top of Braveheart Wall by traversing out right onto the ridge after skiing the top pitch of Chancers. Note this is a different aspect to the slopes above so re-assess whether you think it's stable before skiing it.

18. Dubh Ridge

similar to:	
harder than:	
combine with:	Chancers

In good snow, you can continue all the way down the ridge line from the top of the Braveheart Wall to the bottom of the Braveheart Chair and often find some great tracks in amongst the rock bands.

Sniffing out some untracked pow somewhere near Dubh Ridge

photo www.benthorburn.com | rider Gav MacKay

19. Lochain Sneak Route

There is a rarely skied short gully line hidden away on the far side of the ridge from the top of Braveheart Wall. It doesn't often have enough snow but is something a little different to look out for on the right day. This line will take you down through rocks into the bottom of Coire an Lochain from where you can skirt round the end of the ridge to the bottom of the chair.

Traversing Out

Once you have skied into Coire Dubh the best way to find your way out is to head for the top of the Braveheart Chairlift. From here do a couple more turns before taking a gentle traverse across to skier's left - you are now heading in the right direction to eventually return to the restaurant. Starting from the edge of the Coire Dubh bowl and slightly lower than the top of the chairlift there are a series of permanent way-markers that you can link together to show you a good route out. These markers take you underneath Winger Wall and other slopes all of which can be known to avalanche or shed cornices so keep your wits about you. In risky conditions make sure you keep moving, travel across suspect slopes one at a time, and stop on the tops of ridges rather than in the terrain trap gullies.

There is some fun skiing on the traverse out including Pinball Alley just before you get to the bottom of Nid Ridge. Once you cross over Nid Ridge you should head for the top of the Rob Roy T-bar from where a snow fence marking Rob Roy's Return leads you back to the bottom of Alpha ready for your next lap!

Many a snowboarder has been heard complaining about the traverse out from here being a long and painful experience – if you start a bit higher than skiers do (top of Braveheart Chair or even higher) it will be more pleasant. Try to keep a bit of height above the waymarkers to save having to do any short bootpacks in the places skiers get away with a quick pole or skate.

Easy Gully & The Steeps

As you get off the top of the Summit Tow if you look directly in front of you, past the bull-wheel at the end of the tow, you are looking at the edge of Aonach Mor's second bowl – Coire an Lochain. There is nowhere else in Scotland (or many other places for that matter) that a ski lift takes you directly to the top of such steep skiing terrain and to be honest most of the skiing in this bowl is too steep for the majority of skiers. The easiest route in the bowl is Easy Gully, but this is still a Grade I winter climb and can feel pretty steep at the top in anything but perfect conditions. The other routes described in this bowl all start to be pretty serious and only the most experienced skiers in the best conditions should think about attempting them. Those skiers looking for more accessible terrain should miss out this bowl and head along to Spikes instead.

Right around this corrie there tend to be large cornice build-ups throughout the season so you need to be extremely careful when going to the edge to have a look over. Do not attempt to find these routes in anything other than clear visibility and be aware that many, many avalanches have occurred in this corrie – sluffs on the scarp slopes at the tops of the gullies are particularly common. None of this bowl is within the ski area boundary so you are on your own in the backcountry here. Be warned!

This corrie is also well used by winter climbers so be aware of who may be below you.

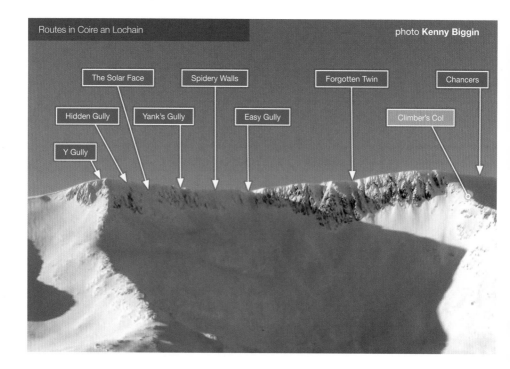

Routes in Coire an Lochain

photo **Kenny Biggin**

The Solar Face · Spidery Walls · Forgotten Twin · Chancers

Hidden Gully · Yank's Gully · Easy Gully · Climber's Col

Y Gully

COIRE AN LOCHAIN

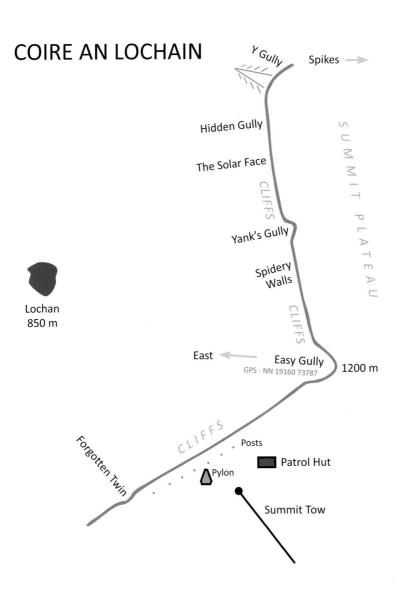

Y Gully

Spikes →

Hidden Gully

The Solar Face

CLIFFS

Yank's Gully

Spidery Walls

SUMMIT PLATEAU

CLIFFS

Lochan
850 m

East ←

Easy Gully
GPS - NN 19160 73787

1200 m

CLIFFS

Posts

Patrol Hut

Forgotten Twin

Pylon

Summit Tow

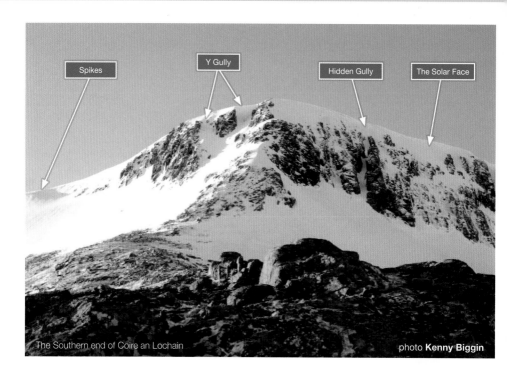

Spikes

Y Gully

Hidden Gully

The Solar Face

The Southern end of Coire an Lochain

photo **Kenny Biggin**

Routes to skier's right of Easy Gully

Hidden Gully

The Solar Face

Yank's Gully

Spidery Walls

Easy Gully

20. Easy Gully

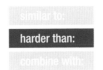

similar to:

harder than: Chancers

combine with:

Easy Gully is the steepest of the 'traditional' lines on Aonach Mor and every good offpiste Scottish skier should aspire to get down it at some point. Having said that it has scared plenty of good skiers and is not really a place to practice falling! If you have skied Chancers a good number of times and feel like you're skiing that easily then Easy Gully should be OK if the snow is forgiving. Sometimes there is a BIG drop off the cornice to get into it and on these days it is not for everyone! It is located around 150m to the right (South) of the Ski Patrol hut and almost always has a big cornice at the top of it. Generally you can get a better look into it from the left hand side though conditions vary. In lean snow years there are actually two gullies – the one on the left can be very narrow hence it's known as 'Squeazy Gully'.

Climbers often use Easy Gully as the 'easy' descent to access the bottom of the many winter climbs in the corrie – try not to sluff snow onto them, trip up on their footsteps, or ski over their ropes - climbers hate that!

photo **Charné Hawkes** | rider **Linn Karlsson**   Ski Patrol watching the drop into Easy Gully

photo **www.benthorburn.com** | rider **Gav MacKay**

Gav MacKay showing that Easy Gully doesn't look so bad after Forgotten Twin!

21. Forgotten Twin

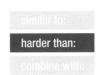

harder than: Hidden Gully

The entrance to Forgotten Twin lies to the left of the top of the Summit Tow and generally there are big cornices everywhere here. It often has climbers in it, has had very few (probably only two) ski descents and is a serious undertaking! Gavin MacKay first skied this line in March 2000, the same day he met his wife – who says romance is dead?!

It's tricky to get a good look down from the top, but pretty important as the main difficulties lie in the middle. There is also often a cliff guarding the exit although there is potential to avoid it to the left (if you're in control).

The first time Gavin skied this line he got a few steep turns in the top section before getting to the middle section which was narrow, icy, and extremely steep. The cliff at the bottom was fairly well covered so he decided to straight-line it. He probably scared the bejeezus out of the two climbers on an adjacent climb – in his own words:

❝ All they would have heard was a bit of scratching around followed by some chimp going at Mach Loonie out into the coire below them.

Gavin skied this scary line again in 2004 and this time his description of the route gives a flavour for what you are getting into.

❝ It was blue bird, beautiful snow and similarly small cornice. I dropped in, boshed out a few beautiful turns on grippy packed pow and then spent the next 10mins picking my way down the centre section. It was a nightmare! Sheet ice, skis bowing ridiculous amounts as I teetered around with tips and tails wedged in the crag either side. I only had about 15ft to get past before she opened out a bit and I could go skiing again but it was buttock clenching stuff.

photo Steven McKenna / Nevis Range
rider Mark Trigg

Mark psyching up for his own Easy Gully backflip sequence

Jonny Pow checking the steep ice is nice and solid for Kenny and Dave Biggin on Spidery Walls in 2009 - Note line of The Solar Face in the background

22. Spidery Walls

5

similar to:

harder than: Easy Gully

combine with:

To the right of Easy Gully there is a steep face before you arrive at Yank's Gully. It is rarely skied but in a good snow year there is a great line (or lines) to be had here. Its name comes from the climbs situated on skier's left – The Web and Spider Rib which at Grade II/III gives you an idea of the steepness here. Be aware that if you fall at the top you will go directly over the cliffs (which would provide great hucking potential if there was deeper snow more often, which there isn't!) There are a couple of variations to skiing this face – essentially you can either break out left (Tarantula) to avoid the cliffs or (more seriously) head rightwards (Black Widow) to drop into a short narrow gully (often steep and broken). There is also a tight line (Funnel-Web) through the middle of the cliff band (skied by Gavin Caruthers in 2012) if you're feeling like a straight line in good conditions. Don't underestimate how steep this face is – steeper than the top of Easy Gully and if you judge the snow wrong it's a scary place to be on ice!

photo **Kenny Biggin**

Climbers at the bottom of Yank's Gully with an impressive cornice up top. Black Widow on the right.

23. Yank's Gully

5

similar to:

harder than: Easy Gully, Y Left

combine with:

A number of people have skied this line thinking (mistakenly) that they were skiing Hidden Gully. It has also been known as Crescent Gully. Mark Hughes and Andy Nelson first skied this as The Funnel back in 1992. The next descent known about was by John 'The Yank' Wrighton back in the mid-90's who jumped in on rental skis and cartwheeled the length of it but came out unscathed. The Yank was followed in by Donald Paterson (with a rope round his waist) and Dave Taylor who managed to stay on their feet. Yank's Gully is an obvious steep gully not far from Easy Gully (whereas Hidden Gully is right along at the very end of the corrie and is, well... hidden!)

The gully cuts through between some famous climbs with Homo Buttress on skier's left and The Prow which has the route Stirling Bridge snaking up it on the right. Yanks is rarely in good enough condition to ski in to from the top without taking a big drop, and the scarp wall more often than not looks like death on a stick with a large cornice to boot. Once you're in the gully isn't dissimilar to Easy Gully, though a bit steeper and narrower.

photo **Kenny Biggin**

Looking across at The Solar Face in the sunrise

24. The Solar Face

similar to:

harder than: Spidery Walls

combine with:

This route is extremely steep, exposed, committing, and full on... but what a line! The entrance to the face lies in between Yank's and Hidden Gully and knowing whether you're in the right place or not at the top is challenge enough since you can't see the whole way down. When you're standing at Easy Gully looking out across the corrie this face looks pretty impressive. Although it looks fairly short both from above and below because of foreshortening, on the face it quickly becomes apparent that this is a big, long, steep line! What's more this route is a strictly no-fall zone as the route out is guarded by a line of cliffs that only sometimes have enough snow to create a (tenuous and tricky to find) small gap through – do not assume you will be able to ski this without either using a rope, taking air, or scaring yourself.

Author's Note: Despite having skied part of this face, I've yet to complete the full line to my satisfaction - conditions are crucial yet elusive. The name comes from the fact that when I get up in the morning and look out of my Spean Bridge kitchen window, this is the route that catches the early solar rays - glinting in the sunshine and taunting me with reminders of scary times!

Jonny Pow taking that all important top turn in his stride (just)

25. Hidden Gully

5	⛰ ⛰ ⛰	similar to:
		harder than: Yank's Gully
		combine with:

Hidden Gully is a classy narrow twisting couloir which appears in the climbing guides as a Grade II winter climb (see photo on front cover). It can be found at the far skier's right hand (Southern) end of Coire an Lochain about 50m before you get to the ridge. As with most of the routes in this corrie it can have a cornice on top with a dangerous and very steep scarp slope. If you fall (or get sluffed) at the top you will be lucky to land anywhere other than hospital! Be warned that although it looks quite short and do-able from the top, it is very foreshortened and feels a lot longer and steeper once you're actually in amongst it… by which time its too late! The top 30metres is the steepest, followed by a rocky narrow section which depending on how much snow there is may or may not be wide enough to squeeze your skis past.

Author's Note: Liam Moynihan & Bob Hyde skied this in 2010 with Bob pointing it from the top! John Sutherland and I (unaware of Liam & Bob's descent) followed a couple of years later, in leaner snow conditions, and made a short film of it called 'Hidden Gully' (find it through the SkiMountain.co.uk website or YouTube). This shows me and John taking half an hour over what took Bob about 10 seconds, but hey… I'm not embarrassed – doing it slow makes for a longer film and anyway, it's turning at the top that's hard ;)

26. Lochan Sector

After sking down Easy Gully or one of the other lines you can ski straight down the fall line to the lochan. However, an alternative is to head right towards the ridge where there is some great terrain up above the lochan on skier's right. You can also access this sector if you cut out to the left after skiing the top of Spikes or the Y Gullies.

Routes out from Coire an Lochain

The route out from Coire an Lochain largely depends on how much snow there is and whether the Braveheart Chair is running. If there is plenty of snow and the chair is running you may as well ski all the way to the bottom, past the lochan and skirt round the bouldery ridge on the left of the corrie which will bring you out just below the bottom of Braveheart.

If there isn't much snow and the chair isn't running then your aim should be to get across to the Coire Dubh bowl high enough so that you can eventually join the normal traverse line. This is sometimes easier said than done, but if you break out to the left after skiing Easy Gully around halfway between the bottom of the crags and the bottom of the corrie and pick your way through bouldery terrain towards a depression in the ridge you will come out in around the right place – the spot to aim for lies at around 900metres, Grid Ref: 199742. Normally you will have to take your skis off a couple of times and perhaps do a short bootpack to get over the ridge. From there you can usually pole and push across to pick up the fifth or sixth traverse line markers.

It is also possible to traverse higher up and cut left immediately under the crags after skiing Easy Gully. Stay as close under the crags as you can and you will come to the end of the corrie just below Climber's Col from where a short bootpack will get you back over into Coire Dubh.

ROUTES OUT FROM THE BACK CORRIES

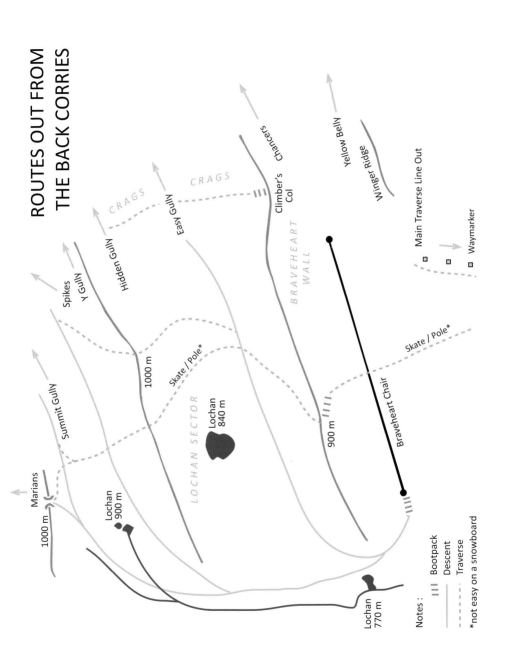

Marians

1000 m

Summit Gully

Lochan
900 m

Spikes

Y Gully

Hidden Gully

CRAGS

Easy Gully

CRAGS

Chancers

Climber's
Col

1000 m

Skate / Pole*

LOCHAN SECTOR

Lochan
840 m

*BRAVEHEART
WALL*

900 m

Braveheart Chair

Skate / Pole*

Yellow Belly

Winger Ridge

Main Traverse Line Out

Waymarker

Lochan
770 m

Notes :

Bootpack

Descent

Traverse

*not easy on a snowboard

Summit Corrie

Further South of the steepness of Coire an Lochain is the more mellow third bowl of Nevis Range. The routes here go virtually from the summit of Aonach Mor at 1221metres and as such (along with the West Face routes) offer some of the longest lift accessed ski descents in Scotland. In order to get to them you have to walk, push, or skin across almost a kilometre of flat, featureless summit plateau and in misty conditions they can be very difficult to find so you should only head out this way if you know where you are going or visibility is extremely good. Although a couple of these routes are marked on Nevis Range's piste map as 'Backcountry Itineraries' they are very much outside the ski area boundary and are unpatrolled, offpiste routes. In misty conditions you should have a map and compass with you to go out this way and know how to use them.

From the ski patrol hut at the top of the Summit Tow you first head across to the top of Easy Gully, skirt round the edge staying well back from the cornice, and then head out across the plateau on a compass bearing of roughly 150 degrees. Depending on what the snow is like it is sometimes worth putting skins on at the ski patrol hut – or if the snow is icy you may well be better poling / skating across. After about half a kilometre you should reach Spikes and from there you can decide whether to ski this or continue on to Summit Gully.

Spikes and Summit Gully – the 3rd bowl of the Back Corries

© SkiMountain

SPIKES & SUMMIT GULLY

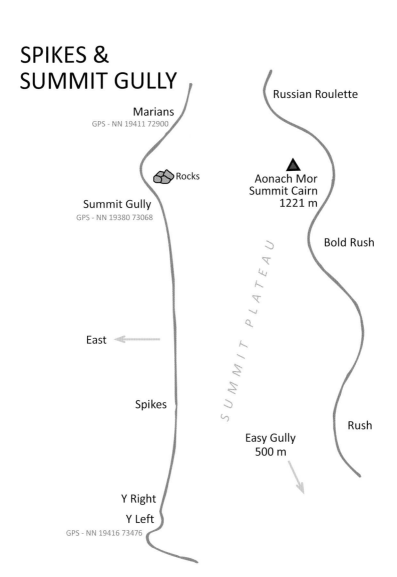

Russian Roulette

Marians
GPS - NN 19411 72900

Rocks

Aonach Mor
Summit Cairn
1221 m

Summit Gully
GPS - NN 19380 73068

Bold Rush

SUMMIT PLATEAU

East

Spikes

Rush

Easy Gully
500 m

Y Right

Y Left
GPS - NN 19416 73476

Summit Gully Rocks

Summit Gully
Alternative Route

Summit Gully

Summit Cairn

Spikes

photo Kenny Biggin

Finding your way in to Summit Gully and Spikes

From Easy Gully an alternative route is to stick close to the edge (not too close!) and follow the ridge round all the way.

Most skiers happy to ski Yellow Belly will also be happy skiing Spikes in the right conditions and with the right people, though navigation is a bigger issue here.

photo Kenny Biggin

The Summit Gully Rocks – the main landmark to look out for in the mist

Donald Paterson testing his edges out in Y Left

27. Y Gully – Y Left

5

similar to:	
harder than:	Easy Gully
combine with:	Lochan Sector

Sitting at the Northern end of this third bowl there is an enticing pair of gullies cutting through a short cliff band in the shape of a 'Y'. They are immediately next to the ridge that takes you into Coire an Lochain and need a fairly good snow year to bring them into condition. They make a more interesting but sometimes very steep start to skiing into this bowl and are not skied often. This line was probably first skied (to the horror of his watching girlfriend) back in the mid nineties by local kayaking legend Andy Jackson. Y Left is quite an obvious gully which can often be steep and rocky at the top but then quickly opens out into the bowl below.

Author's Note: The first time I met the late Andy Jackson we skied a very icy Summit Gully together - he fell and lost a ski near the top and almost took me out after a long and scary slide... I can still remember him skeetering fast towards me with flailing arms yelling 'Caaatch Meee...!'

28. Y Right

harder than: Y Left

Just to skier's right of Y Left there is a route through the rocks. This line is more of a short face than a gully and is generally steeper and more exposed than Y Left. This route will probably mainly appeal to those who want to leave no line unskied!

29. Spikes

similar to: Yellow Belly

Originally known as Spike's Fright, this route got it's name in the early '80s when a few folk had hiked up with skis to investigate what the skiing would be like if a new resort were to be built here. Very few (if any) people had skied any of the Back Corries at that time but Spike (Ian Sykes) took a look over the edge and thought 'Hey, that looks OK that does!'. His buddies (including fellow Nevis Range directors Ian 'Sudsy' Sutherland and Ian Milton) had their doubts but encouraged him never the less. Full of confidence, Spike jumped off the cornice and proceeded to be the first person to tomahawk down the slope – much to everyone else's amusement! Perhaps this was the real start to offpiste skiing at Nevis Range…

Spikes as it is usually called now, is an open bowl stretching from the edge of the cliffs leading to the Coire an Lochain ridge and along to the start of Summit Gully. There can be a cornice at the top of Spikes but it is generally seen as an easier option than Summit Gully and a superb 'first adventure' beyond the ski area boundary. It is tricky to find the top in bad visibility so save this for a blue sky day unless you know where you're going.

photo Charné Hawkes

One of the best and most accessible backcountry runs in Scotland – Spikes

After dropping into Spikes at the top there is a fantastic long pitch of open offpiste skiing. If the chair isn't running or you fancy staying high, you can cut left out of Spikes after around 200metres. Here there is a small col leading over the ridge into Coire an Lochain and from here it is possible to traverse round and eventually join the main traverse line out from Corrie Dubh.

For the full run you carry on all the way down the fall line, eventually passing a small snow covered lochan at 900metres. From the lochan there are a few different lines with the most obvious being to follow the open gully line down with one slightly steeper pitch before it flattens out as you come underneath Coire an Lochain. Carry on across the flat section until you come to another small lochan and shortly after this a 20metre bootpack leads you to the bottom of the Braveheart Chair.

photo **Kenny Biggin**

Looking into Summit Gully

30. Summit Gully

3

similar to:	
harder than:	Spikes
combine with:	The Far Side

Summit Gully is right at the end of Aonach Mor's third bowl and this traditionally marks the end of the Back Corries area. It is a wide and open gully sitting between the ridge at the end of the bowl and a loosely defined area that takes you into Spikes. In the right conditions Summit Gully is without doubt one of the finest and longest lift served offpiste runs in Scotland.

Many people have got lost for a while trying to find the top of Summit Gully – there are some distinctive rocks marking the top though these could become buried if there is a lot of snow. The important thing is not to go beyond the ridge (see Marians) – the ridge should be on your right on the way down!

Summit Gully contains three distinct sections and it's worth bearing in mind that the steepest bit (though not by much) is often at the start of the middle section. At the very end of the season a bergschrund sometimes opens up in this middle section, though it is usually easy to get round. As the gully opens out and flattens at the bottom keep your speed up and continue gently down the fall line across the corrie. Eventually the run takes you into one last steeper section before spilling you out into the valley floor below Coire an Lochain.

photo **Kenny Biggin**

Pristine tracks in Summit Gully

For those looking for air, there is some good small cliff-huckage and windlip potential in the Summit Gully area, and a variety of different lines to be explored at the top of the route.

31. The Far Side

similar to: Braveheart

harder than:

combine with:

When the snow is good, the lifts are busy (rare!), and you have your touring kit with you one option is to ski down Summit Gully but then cut out to the right to a col on the ridge half-way down. From here you can put your skins on and get up onto the ridge of Stob a Chul-Choire. It can make a nice ski if you traverse round from here towards Tom na Sroine and then ski back into the corrie towards the bottom of the Braveheart Chairlift.

There are also a couple of enticing routes going off the steep East face of Tom na Sroine but these are adventure skiing and will require a long hike out whichever way you look at it.

photo **Kenny Biggin** | riders **Donald Paterson
Kenny Grant,
John Sutherland**

On top of Stob a Chul-Choire on the way to The Far Side. Spikes in the background

ROSSIGNOL

An Cul Choire

In between Summit Gully and the Aonach Beag col there is a kilometre wide corrie to the East with some great backcountry terrain in it. This area hardly ever gets skied but should really be seen as the 'fourth bowl' of the Back Corries (especially as An Cul Choire translates as The Back Corrie). For the non-Gaelic speakers amongst us, An Cul Choire is usually pronounced roughly 'Ankle Corrie'. If you don't mind skinning or hiking out, this area provides some good options to head for if Summit Gully gets tracked out.

AN CUL CHOIRE

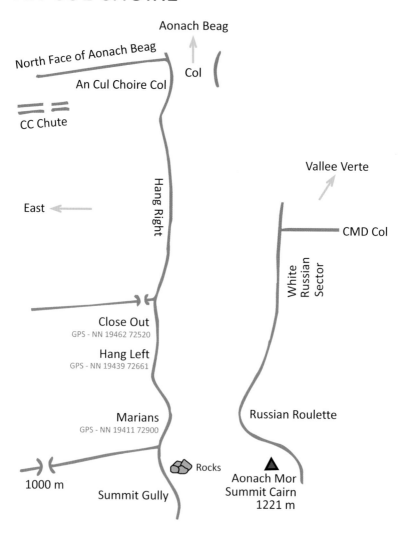

Cul Choire Col

Hang Right

Close Out

Hang Left

Marians

Summit Gully

Routes into An Cul Choire

photo **Kenny Biggin**

32. Marians

3

similar to: Summit Gully

~~harder than~~

~~combine with~~

This route was pioneered unintentionally in the mist by Nevis Range MD Marian Austin – it's better to do it on a clear day unless you know exactly where you are going! If you ski past Summit Gully and past the Summit Gully rocks you end up on the far side of Aonach Mor's East Ridge above a large bowl that eventually spills out into the catchment for the River Cour.

If you don't want a long hike or skin out, you can still ski the top couple of hundred metres of Marians and then traverse left to get to a col that brings you into the lower part of Summit Gully – if the Braveheart Chair isn't running this col is still (just) high enough to do a long traverse back from if you do a good job of staying high and don't mind a bit of poling and skating.

Skinning back up the lower half of Marians out from An Cul Choire

photo **Neil Fleming** | rider **Katie Fleming**

If you decide to go all the way down, follow the fall line down the initial three hundred metres of the bowl, but then stay to your left to avoid some small cliffs. At this point the angle eases off a bit and by turning rightwards you join the broad gully holding the top of the Allt a' Chul Choire burn. Follow this gully line in a roughly South-Easterly direction picking your way between the rocks. If there isn't enough snow there are a series of small waterfalls to negotiate in the lower section of the run, but it is usually possible to pick your way down and with good cover there is excellent skiing all the way to the bottom.

33. Hang Left

similar to:	Marians
harder than:	
combine with:	

The next bowl along from Marians is similar in character and gives a couple of hundred metres of nice riding before you need to cut left to join Marians to avoid the cliffs.

Looking across to Aonach Beag and the Cul Choire Col with the pristine slopes of Close Out and Hang Left on the right

photo **Kenny Biggin**

34. Close Out

4

About halfway between the Aonach Mor summit and the Aonach Beag col the corrie is split by a rocky spine. There is good skiing to be had on skier's left of this spine for a while but be ready to stop and bootpack back up because there is no easy way down through the cliffs at the bottom.

Author's Note: The day I skied this route the visibility was bad but I got down around 300m (of rutted ice) before arriving at a band of cliffs. There is a small inviting gully on the right but at that point visibility lowered to zero percent with wind howling up the face leaving me with little choice but to put my crampons on, get my axe out and hike out. If you decide to explore this line and get further than I did, share the story with us via the SkiMountain facebook page!

35. Spine Chute

To skier's right of the rocky spine that splits this corrie there is a pleasing little chute that makes a more exciting alternative to skiing from the Aonach Beag col. It takes a fair amount of snow to make this skiable. Get to the top of the chute by skiing the first couple of turns of Close Out and traverse right to a minor col on the spiny ridge.

36. Hang Right

combine with: CC Chute

In between the rocky spine and the Aonach Beag col, there are a variety of sweet lines of varying difficulties taking you into the top of the Cul Choire bowl. There is a large band of cliffs below this section so after skiing the top 300metres you have to hang a right to where you can drop into the CC Chute.

37. Cul Choire Col

similar to: Yellow Belly

harder than: Backtrack

combine with: The Grey Corries

Leading down to the East from the Aonach Mor / Aonach Beag col there is a great descent into the headwaters of the River Cour. As with Marians, this is a good way to begin a trip along the Grey Corries. It also makes a nice trip to ski down here and then skin back up the lower half of Marians to the col that brings you back into Summit Gully and from there head back to the lifts.

The run starts from the Aonach Beag col with a large open bowl which usually has an 'easy' way in if you look around – although the top has a bit of steepness to it, this quickly mellows. After around 200metres of descent with the impressive cliffs of the North East Ridge of Aonach Beag on your right you can choose whether to enter the CC Chute or stick to the easier slopes on the right which lead all the way down to the valley floor.

38. CC Chute

3

similar to:

harder than:

combine with:

Halfway down the ski into An Cul Choire from the Aonach Beag col, you have the option of dropping into a spectacular hanging couloir. It is quite an unusual feature so has a great novelty factor (where else is there a couloir in the middle of a bowl like this?). The couloir is in two sections with the first section being shorter and slightly easier – if you didn't enjoy the first section you can break out right and meet your buddies at the bottom. Be aware that if there isn't enough snow or it's late season the bottom part of this gully is a waterfall.

photo **Kenny Biggin**

Freeride heaven - Cul Choire Col, Hang Right, and the CC Chute. East Face of Aonach Beag far left, Close Out far right

Routes Out from An Cul Choire

Once down in the bottom of this large glen you are surrounded by big mountains – the Aonachs behind you with the Grey Corries stretching out in front. It feels like you are in the middle of nowhere, because in many respects you are! The easiest way out of here is to skin back up the lower slopes of Marians to the Stob an Cul Choire col at Grid Ref: 198731. This col takes you into Summit Gully about halfway down and (even if Braveheart isn't running) if you keep your height and do a bit of poling / skating it is possible from here to traverse all the way back to the lifts without walking (depending on snow cover of course).

When skinning up Marians there can be a couple of steeper sections beside waterfalls which may require short bootpacks depending on snow. You can also skin back up to the Aonach Beag col but from there you have to go back over the summit of Aonach Mor.

Another option is to follow the Allt a Chul Choire / Allt Coire an Eoin burn all the way out but be warned that it isn't recommended as it can feel like a LONG way with little gradient to keep you sliding, even if there is snow this low down. If you decide you do want to go this way you will eventually come to the dam at the start of the River Cour. From here you can follow the forest road and after around 1.5km pick up the puggy line which (if you've planned ahead!) will take you back to your parked car at the top of the Corriechoille road (Grid Ref: 256788). In lots of snow you can also follow paths and tracks all the way back to Spean Bridge, (or the Nevis Range car park for that matter) but it's a long way! Although the Corriechoille road isn't a public road, at the time of writing there is usually no objection to parking your car here, so long as you do so responsibly.

The West Side

With all the amazing skiing on offer in the Back Corries, it's easy to forget that this mountain has two sides to it! When the snow is right there is some great skiing here though, so read on…

700 m Vallee Verte

300 m White Russian Sector

Russian Roulette
GPS - NN 19322 72824

AONACH MOR
WEST FACE

Aonach Mor
Summit Cairn
GPS - NN 19300 72950

Don't Rush
GPS - NN 19245 72967

Grotto Rush
GPS - NN 19210 73018

Bold Rush
GPS - NN 19291 73117

West

Rush
GPS - NN 19247 73363

Looking across at the West Face of Aonach Mor from Carn Mor Dearg's North Ridge

39. The Vallee Verte

Like its famous alpine cousin, The Vallee Blanche (in Chamonix), the Vallee Verte is a long and rewarding trip that takes you through some spectacular and remote scenery. Although there is enough angle to keep good skiers happy the route never gets stupidly steep so in good snow conditions should be achievable by most people who are happy skiing the Back Corries, especially if accompanied by more experienced skiers or guides. Unfortunately as the name suggests (The Green Valley) there is often more grass than snow on the lower part of the run because it largely faces South so melts early. If you get a chance to do this run when there is snow all the way down it is an epic trip. The route takes you from the summit of Aonach Mor all the way to the car park at the end of the road in Glen Nevis – the best way to do this is to leave a car at this car park beforehand.

From the top of the Summit Tow go across the plateau to the Aonach Mor summit cairn. Continue past the cairn in a Southerly direction for about 700metres on gentle slope at which point you pass the indistinct ridge coming up from Carn Mor Dearg hidden below you on your right. Providing you're doing this in good visibility (highly recommended!) you should be able to see all the way down the glen from here and across to the Meall Cumhann col. Instead of continuing down the gentle slope to the Aonach Beag col you can drop into the bowl on your right (SW from around Grid Ref: 191722) and pick your line down towards the bottom of the glen. If there isn't loads of snow there is often a tricky band of slabby rocks near the bottom of this pitch, but you can find a route through by traversing far right or left.

photo **Kenny Biggin**
rider **Dave Biggin**

Grass skiing down from Meall Cumhann at the end of the Vallee Verte

From here the corrie flattens out and you have two choices:

- **Giubhsachan** – stick to the stream bed and skate over the long flat section. After the flat section the route steepens a little again for the last few hundred metres (often a walk or steep grass ski) which follows the Allt Coire Giubhsachan out to the Old Steall ruins. From there it is a 2.5km walk out – first along to the wire bridge, then across Steall meadows and out along the good path that leads through the gorge to the car park.

- **Meall Cumhann** – rather than endure the walk out from Old Steall you can try to keep your height after the rock band and aim for the Meall Cumhann col instead (Grid Ref: 178700). In good snow you can just about make the col on skis with a traverse but usually you will need to do a short bootpack to get there. Once over the col traverse across to the right for around half a kilometre before dropping down steeply towards the car park. If you've chosen the right day you will be able to ski all the way to the car, but many times this will be either a steep walk down or a fairly extreme grass ski (take care!). You can also drop directly down the fall line and through the trees to pick up the Steall gorge path. If there is lots and lots of snow you may even have to leave your car at the lower falls carpark at Polldubh and ski back to it along the road!

The Rush Face (The West Face)

The West Face of Aonach Mor is hidden away over to your right as you go up the main ski tows. This side of the mountain doesn't get as much snow as the Back Corries on the East and is often ignored. However, there are some epic runs to be had here so if you think conditions are right and you want an adventure why not take a look? Knowing which gully is which on this face is notoriously tricky and many a conversation along the following lines has been overheard even amongst Nevis Range locals:

" Have you skied Bold Rush?"

" Which one is that?"

" I'm never sure whether it's the one next to the summit"

" No is that one not Don't Rush where you need to abseil?"

" Hmm, I'm not sure actually – the one we skied ten years ago was great though… but I can't quite remember where it was!"

Hopefully the following section will put the debate to rest, though inevitably it may become the subject of many more bar-side conversations to come! Because it is not possible to see the bottom or full length of any of these routes from the top you must either be 100% sure about where you are or you must be prepared and equipped for things to get steep and potentially have to either climb back up, or abseil down at the bottom. Taking ice axe and crampons as a minimum is recommended on the West Face, as is starting with the easiest route (Rush) and then working your way up to the harder ones after scoping them out from the bottom.

Summit Cairn

Bold Rush

Rush

Finding Rush and Bold Rush

40. Ground Rush Sector

5

Similar to:

harder than:

combine with:

Running along the West Face from about three quarters of the way up the Quad Chairlift up to about half way up the Summit Tow, there are a number of nice looking gully lines. Unfortunately they all end in a band of slabby cliffs which make skiing these lines seem like a bit of a waste of time. Perhaps in an exceptional snow year some of these lines will fill in and become skiable top to bottom – failing that, they are best left alone as the rest of the West Face gullies are classier by far.

The Rush Face

41. Rush

3

harder than: Summit Gully

This is the easiest full length route on the face and was named (along with Bold Rush and Don't Rush) 'back in the day' by some of the early avalanche service guys (Mark Hughes and Graham Moss). This isn't really a gully as such – it has a reasonably open and wide feel and should be most people's introduction to skiing on the West Face. Providing the snow is in reasonable condition there won't be too many nasty surprises going down Rush, although it is still a steep run and the steepness is sustained for the length of the run (around 400m!). Assuming the snow conditions are soft it is within the capabilities of anyone who has skied Chancers or Summit Gully and felt comfortable – however when snow conditions are less than ideal this is not a place to fall! Depending on snow cover there may be a few rocks or slightly tricky steps towards the bottom of Rush, but these can usually be avoided fairly easily by traversing out one way or the other.

Don't Rush

Grotto Rush

Bold Rush

photo **Kenny Biggin**

Looking in from the top right of Bold Rush. Powder anyone?

42. Bold Rush

4

similar to:	Easy Gully
harder than:	Rush
combine with:	Carn Mor Dearg

This is the most well known route on the West Face but even then it isn't skied often. Bold Rush is also known as Downhill Gully and Soldier's Gully in the climbing guides. It is very often confused with Rush as the entrance looks very similar – both entrances are wide curved rolling convex depressions in the western rim of the summit plateau. As the names suggest – you can rush down Rush, but Bold Rush can be a bit trickier.

Bold Rush is the one closer to the Summit. This is arguably the classiest gully on the whole mountain as it is just narrow enough, just steep enough, and plenty long enough to put the likes of Easy Gully to shame.

Powder in Bold Rush

photo **Kenny Biggin**

Bold Rush can be found on the right (West) about 50metres before you reach the summit cairn of Aonach Mor. Even after galeforce Easterly winds the tops of these gullies are rarely corniced and instead roll over in a convex fashion making it tricky to get a good look into them without committing. As always be wary of avalanches. Just as dangerous on this face is slipping on ice – all the routes here are long and sustained so make sure the snow is forgiving.

At the end of Bold Rush there is often a short steeper and narrower section – this varies widely with conditions and can be anything from a short icy step to a huge bank of snow. There is usually a way through (especially for good skiers) but you may want to take axe and crampons with you just in case.

photo **Dave Biggin** | rider **Kenny Biggin**

Opening out after a run down Bold Rush

© SkiMountain

photo **Kenny Biggin** | rider **Dave Biggin**

What a run... Halfway down Bold Rush

43. Grotto Rush

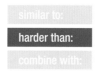

harder than: Bold Rush

(aka Cave Gully in the climbing guides)

A route for solid skiers in good conditions, for those capable enough this is a real classic. The entrance lies just to the right of the summit and immediately to the left of the large rock spine that makes the left wall of Bold Rush. If you start too far to the left you will end up in Don't Rush instead.

This is a steep 400m couloir divided in two by a short ice pitch with a large cave. There is a vague possibility that the ice pitch could be skied in the right conditions but it's hardly a place to take a risk. When you come to the ice pitch there is no easing of gradient but there is a large flake on the ridge on skiers right which provides a reassuring and easy belay using a long sling. If you are confident enough you will be able to set up the belay and do the rap while keeping your skis on (slide down the steep section backwards!) Only the bravest will venture into the cave as there are whispered legends of a dark force living here with a penchant for shiny ski equipment!

From the cave the gully continues to be classy, steep and narrow (but never extreme) until it spits you out the bottom with a smile on your face.

photo **Kenny Biggin** | rider **John Sutherland**

Looking into the top of Grotto Rush

photo **Kenny Biggin** | rider **John Suth...**

Checking out the short ice pitch in Grotto Rush

What lies within? Feeling a presence outside the cave in Grotto Rush

44. Don't Rush

harder than: Bold Rush

Don't Rush (also known as 3Rap Rush, or Easter Gully in the climbing guides) is a fantastic narrow couloir snaking off almost directly beneath the summit cairn. The entrance is a short traverse to skier's left away from the top of Bold Rush with Grotto Rush in between. It's a great ski but some would say it's an even better abseil – either way, it's a fantastic adventure!

After skiing the narrow twisting gully for around 300metres you come to an obvious horizon line and from here you need to set up anchors and abseil down around 100metres of ice fall (3 rappels using two 30m ropes) – this ice fall is in the climbing guides as Spare Rib Gully (Grade III). Only good skiers prepared to ski in control (on 40-45 degrees) down to the edge and then switch to full on mountaineering mode should attempt this route – you will need crampons, ice axe, 2 x 30metre ropes, harness, plus enough gear to set up anchors in the rock or ice for three abseils (you may well need to sacrifice some gear to set up safe rap anchors).

photo **Kenny Biggin** | rider **Donald Paterson**

Perfect snow at the top of Don't Rush

Enjoying the abseil as much as the ski – the escape
from Don't Rush

45. Russian Roulette

similar to:

harder than: Grotto Rush

combine with:

This is another long and committing couloir whose entrance is around 50metres past (South of) the summit cairn. The line is made all the more exciting (or scary depending on your viewpoint) by the sure knowledge that you can't ski directly out the bottom of it. There is a 10metre ice fall guarding the exit at the bottom which you will either need to abseil down or you can try to ski out by breaking out of the gully to the left just above the icefall. If you decide to abseil, make sure you are ready to set up anchors – there is no easy place to stop and do this so practise your routine somewhere less scary first!

Most skiers attempting this will prefer to try to ski out along the long and exposed traverse to the left which you gain access to just before the top of the ice fall, but this is where the 'Russian Roulette' element comes in as you probably only have a 50/50 chance (if that!) of being able to ski out – you may well need to take a bullet and change (on steep ground) to crampons and axe, or even get a rope out, in order to escape along the traverse so be ready. The best advice is to take a very good look at the exit of this route from the bottom before making an attempt.

Possible line of escape from Russian Roulette

Russian Roulette

looking down from halfway

exit?

ROTTEFELLA®

Powered by you.
Technology by us.

The Rottefella Freeride binding provides
you with optimal grip from edge to edge and
excellent control on hard and icy surfaces.

mountainboot.co.uk

46. White Russian Sector

similar to:	
harder than:	
combine with:	Carn Mor Dearg

If you go beyond the summit cairn and the obvious opening of Russian Roulette for around 300metres there are a number of shorter but less well defined West Face lines. They generally get shorter and easier the further you get from the summit, though be warned that this is still steep ground. Don't be tempted to drop off the ridge too close to the summit as there are still plenty of cliffs in this area. If conditions are suitable, this is a good way to get to the Carn Mor Dearg col for an ascent of the South East Ridge. The first line to be skied in this area was probably by Spike and Sudsy in the mid-eighties with the Allt Daim bursting at the seams with snow.

Routes Out from The West Face

There are three options to get out from the West Face:

Chairlift

The most obvious option for getting out from the West Face is via a 30minute hike out to the chairlift. Ski as far as you can along the right bank of the Allt Daim burn. Your aim is to get as close as you can to the col (Grid Ref: 178753) between Aonach Mor's West Ridge and Meall Beag. Don't go too high too early as there are some nasty rock slabs that you need to skirt round the bottom of. The best line is usually to keep going down the burn line until you are almost under the col, and then walk (or skin) up towards it. Skirting under the last rocky slab you pick up a rough path that has been worn by climbers coming down from the col. If there is lots of snow treat this slope with caution – if icy you may need crampons and it has been known to avalanche. Once you reach the col you can easily join the path that leads back to the bottom of the chairlift and head back up for another run!

All the way down

If you don't fancy the half hour hike back up towards Meall Beag and the chairlift (or if there is loads of snow or you suspect you're too late to get the last Gondola) you may want to ski on down the glen until you come to the dam across the burn – from here there is a track leading down into the forest and eventually back to the Nevis Range car park. This is quite a long way though so the hike back to the chair is usually a better option.

Carn Mor Dearg

If you are feeling fit and the snow is in good nic, why not combine a trip down the West Face with a hike or skin up onto Carn Mor Dearg (see next section).

Carn Mor Dearg

Few good skiers can have been at Nevis Range on a blue sky day and not gazed longingly across at the pristine bowls of the East side of Carn Mor Dearg. Despite this it gets skied surprisingly rarely... perhaps this is because you are looking at a minimum ascent of around 500metres followed by a further effort to extricate yourself having skied it. It's well worth the trip though so get yourself up there.

The main routes up are either by skiing across from the bottom of the Quad Chairlift, and then bootpacking or skinning up the main North ridge. Or an alternative is to ski down a line on the Rush Face and then up the steep and alpine ridge sitting at the Southern end of the mountain. You can also skin up either side of the broad flank of the North Ridge from the Blue Crane or from the upper North Face car park.

Approach from Chairlift

From the bottom of the chairlift follow the path across towards Meall Beag, or better still go up the chairlift, and ski across from near the bottom of the Far West piste. Head for the col just South of Meall Beag at Grid Ref: 178753. Depending on how much snow there is ski or walk down the slope towards the Allt Daim, cross over the burn and climb steeply up onto the North Ridge. Be aware that although you are low down, this route still takes you over potential avalanche slopes. The North Ridge tends to hold a strip of snow along its Eastern edge just wide enough to skin up long after the rest of this side of the hill has melted. If it's icy you may need harscheisen or crampons to get all the way up as there are a couple of steeper sections.

The East Ridge of Carn Mor Dearg with classic skiing either side and Tower Gully behind

photo **Kenny Biggin**

Approach from Blue Crane

If the Gondola is shut and you're feeling fit, you can gain access to Carn Mor Dearg by following the forest road from the Nevis Range car park up to the Aluminium Smelter hydroelectric intake at Grid Ref: 162759. There used to be a blue crane here that has since been removed but the name sticks. The track fords across the burn here and continues for another 500metres to a dam. From here you have around 700metres of height gain to get to the first top (Carn Beag Dearg). From the dam, follow the burn for a few hundred metres until it starts to get gorge-like and then strike up the ridge in a Southerly direction.

Approach from North Face Car Park

It's a long slog but you may find a reason to approach from the North Face car park. If so, follow the North Face path from the top car park for around a kilometre before striking out across the open hillside to the East. With enough snow you can skin up here relatively easily but this face tends not to hold onto snow for very long.

Approach from CIC Hut

If you're combining a trip up Carn Mor Dearg with a ski on Ben Nevis, or perhaps a stay in the CIC Hut, there are a variety of routes open to you depending on how much snow there is. A steep but direct option is to go straight up the West Face, while a gentler skinning line takes you across to the left and up the broad shoulder. Another alternative for the adventurous is to skin up into Coire Leis and scramble across the Carn Mor Dearg Arete.

photo **Dougie Pryce**

The big Carn Mor Bowl of Carn Mor Dearg looking stonking with the South East Ridge and CMD Arete on the left, Ben Nevis behind

© SkiMountain

Approach from Rush Face

By far the classiest way to access Carn Mor Dearg is to ski a line on the West Face of Aonach Mor – perhaps Rush, Bold Rush, or one of the White Russian lines – and then skin / bootpack up the South East ridge. Once you're out of the bottom of your Rush Face line, traverse or skin across to the Aonach Mor / Carn Mor Dearg col at Grid Ref: 187722. The ridge is quite steep in places so a mixture of skins with harscheisen and crampons / axe will probably be needed. It's a great outing up this ridge in snowy conditions so this is a highly recommended approach option (though definitely trickier and more exposed than going up the North Ridge). This ridge takes you out more or less at the summit of Carn Mor Dearg from where you can pick your route down!

Once at the top you have a choice of three large bowls on the East Face – all with excellent skiing to be had though big cornices and avalanches on this face are not uncommon.

photo **Kenny Biggin**
rider **John Sutherland**

Skinning up the South East Ridge of Carn Mor Dearg

Ben Nevis

Carn Mor Dearg

Carn Mor Bowl

Meadhonach Bowl

Carn Beag Bowl

SE Ridge

photo **John Sutherland**

The Carn Mor Dearg Bowls looking rocky. Taken from the West Face of Aonach Mor with Grotto Rush to the left and Bold Rush to the right

47. Carn Beag Bowl

2

similar to:	Yellow Belly
harder than:	
combine with:	

Beyond the Carn Beag Dearg top at 1010metres lies the lowest and easiest bowl which often remains less filled in than the other two higher bowls. Those who want a shorter hike or an easier ski may well choose to drop into this bowl while the purists will want to go further along the ridge.

"There are few things better than finally riding a sweet line you've been looking at for years!"

Looking into Carn Beag Bowl

48. Meadhonach Bowl

similar to:	Chancers
harder than:	
combine with:	Ben Nevis or The Rush Face

This is the middle bowl of Carn Mor Dearg's East Face, with Carn Dearg Meadhonach (1179metres) at its Southern end. The bowl stretches for over half a kilometre and has some fantastic skiing in it. There is a particularly good steeper line coming down close to the impressive ridge at the South end of this bowl, but it is possible to drop in anywhere along its length. The Northern end (skier's left) is generally easier with some very forgiving entrances on offer if you make use of the ridge where there are less cornices. Remember to take some time to take a good look across at the routes on the West Face of Aonach Mor from here as this is probably one of the best vantage points.

49. Carn Mor Bowl

similar to:	
harder than:	
combine with:	Ben Nevis or The Rush Face

The third and highest bowl with the Carn Mor Dearg summit at 1220metres at its head again has a myriad of nice lines to choose from, including some (much) more intense lines picking your way amongst the summit cliffs at the Southern end if that's your bag. As with the Meadhonach Bowl, the easier lines are found at the Northern end of the bowl where it's possible to ski in next to the ridge without significant steepness. The middle of the bowl has a wide variety of entrance options, with some big cornices being a common feature. The Carn Mor Bowl is probably one of the most interesting corries in the area from the point of view of freeride potential, with many different options for linking drops, gullies, and ribs. Remember that you will be being watched by the skiers at Nevis Range and that your tracks (or wipeout evidence) will be on show for all to see - no pressure!

photo **Dougie Pryce**

Carn Mor Bowl looking tasty

Neil Muir getting psyched up to rip down a classic heather pillow line on the North Ridge of Carn Mor Dearg.

photo **Kenny Biggin** | rider **Neil Muir**

Routes out from the East Face of Carn Mor Dearg

The bottom of all three bowls tends to be quite rocky so take care making your way down to the Allt Daim burn. With luck there will be enough snow to ski along the burn to a point where you can hike back up to the Meall Beag col and from there follow the path back to the chairlift (see Routes out from Aonach Mor West Face). The alternative is to continue all the way down the burn (the East bank on skier's right is more forgiving in general) until you get to the dam and then follow the forest track back to the Nevis Range car park, but this is a long slog unless there is lots of snow.

50. Carn Mor Dearg West Face

similar to:	SCB South Face
harder than:	
combine with:	Rush

Although it tends not to have loads of snow on it, it can also be a good ski to continue over the far side of Carn Mor Dearg and ski down the West Face towards the CIC Hut. It is over 500metres down to the CIC Hut and the views across to the North Face of the Ben are great, so when there's enough snow this is well worth a trip. You can drop off the ridge anywhere along its length although obviously the longest ski is from the summit. The West Face is a good open ski that keeps going but never gets too steep. If there is enough snow you may even be able to ski all the way past the CIC Hut and on down to the top or even bottom North Face car parks, though obviously you will then need a lift from here to get back to Nevis Range.

51. Triple Crown

A classic (if long) trip is to combine Carn Mor Dearg with a ski on Ben Nevis and Aonach Mor. There are many different flavours of this excellent combination trip, but the 'traditional classic' goes like this:

- Hike / skin up the Ben Nevis Mountain Track / Red Burn
- Ski Tower Gully
- Skin up the West Face of Carn Mor Dearg
- Ski the East Face of Carn Mor Dearg via the Carn Mor Bowl
- Hike up to the summit of Aonach Mor via the CMD col (or the chairlift)
- Then ski either Easy Gully or Summit Gully for a pretty unbeatable day!
- Finish in the bar at the Snowgoose Restaurant

You can tailor the Triple Crown to suit snow conditions and your tastes, for instance if Tower Gully looks a little spicy you can exchange it for something like Number 4 or the Abseil Posts route in Coire Leis. Likewise you can do a 'Reverse Triple Crown' by starting up the lifts at Nevis Range, then skiing the West Face of Aonach Mor, up the East Ridge of Carn Mor Dearg, down the West Face of Carn Mor Dearg, up Ledge Route (or similar) and down The Red Burn on Ben Nevis.

End of season turns in the Calm Couloir on Aonach
Beag's East Face

photo **Kenny Biggin**

The exit chute below the Mercy and Mor Couloirs
on Aonach Beag's West Face

photo **Kenny Biggin**

Aonach Beag

Aonach Beag is the spectacular mountain that lies 2.5km South of the top of the Summit Tow. Despite or perhaps because of its proximity to Nevis Range it gets skied surprisingly rarely which is a shame because it has some of the best freeride terrain in Scotland!

photo **Dougie Pryce** | rider **Reamonn Lenkas**

Bootpacking up Aonach Beag from the col with Aonach Mor

A good day to soak up the views on the summit of
Aonach Beag

52. Beag and Back

Going across to the summit of Aonach Beag and back is a great little ski tour in itself, and provides
a good familiarisation exercise if you're new to this side of the mountains. This is more of a journey
than an offpiste descent but it's well worth doing.

From the top of the Summit Tow skin, walk or skate across to the Aonach Mor summit cairn. From
here ski down the fairly gentle slope to the South, staying on the ridge with An Cul Choire on your left
and the White Russian sector of the Rush Face on your right. The Aonach Mor / Aonach Beag col is
at Grid Ref: 193718. From here it will depend on snow conditions whether you can skin all the way
up or not. In some conditions crampons may be required though if they are you might question how
good the ski back is going to be. The trickiest part of the ridge comes first – in the right snow picking

Southwest Faces of Ben Nevis and Aonach Beag from Mullach nan Coirean. Red Burn far left

photo **Kenny Biggin** | rider **Neil Muir**

Skiing off the summit of Aonach Beag at the start of
the South Face

your way between the rock band on skins is reasonably doable. Many will need to take skis off to get
through the rocks.

Continue up the ridge staying well away from the big cornices that form on the left (East) side. The
summit area in particular is known for forming huge cornices so stay well away from the edge. Take
in the view, take some photos and then ski back!

53. Aonach Beag South Face

     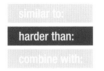

similar to:

harder than: SCB South Face

combine with:

From the summit of Aonach Beag you can get almost 1000metres of 'vert' skiing down the South
Face into Glen Nevis. Apart from a small flattish section around halfway down (where you can let
your legs recover) the gradient stays good for most offpiste skiers all the way down. It's just a shame
it's South facing so tends not to have enough snow, and of course there is a half hour walk (or skin)
out from the Steall ruins across the meadows and through the gorge to the car park at the bottom.

From the summit you ski in a Southerly direction and after 100metres or so the gradient picks up a
little as you drop into a large open bowl – there are a range of lines here with some being steeper
than others but it is easy to find a fairly gentle line the whole way. After around 400metres of descent
there is a plateau area and from here you follow the burn line all the way down to Steall ruins.

You will need to leave a car at the top car park in Glen Nevis (or at the lower falls if the road is
snowed under!) Don't rely on phoning for a lift from here as there is generally no mobile reception.

54. SCB South Face

similar to:

harder than:

combine with:

A slightly easier angled variation to Aonach Beag's South Face is to ski down the ridge from the summit and after passing the entrance to the Calm Couloir skirt round to the left below Stob Coire Bhealaich. Traverse to the East for a short way and then continue down easy slopes in a South Westerly direction, eventually meeting up with the South Face route and following the lower section of the Allt Coire nan Laogh burn down to Steall ruins in Glen Nevis.

photo **Ron Cameron** | rider **Russell Leaper**

Stopping for a breather on the SCB South Face

photo **Ron Cameron** | rider **Russell Leaper**

You know you've picked the right day for a trip down into Glen Nevis if you can't get the car up the road! After skiing the SCB South Face

Aonach Beag West Face

Hidden from view from most places except the Vallee Verte and the top of Ben Nevis, there are three tempting gullies in amongst the crags of the West Face of Aonach Beag.

Routes on the West Face of Aonach Beag

photo **Kenny Biggin**

AONACH BEAG WEST FACE

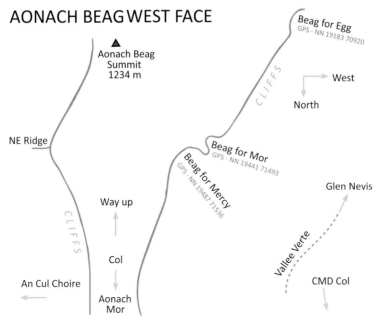

▲
Aonach Beag
Summit
1234 m

NE Ridge

Beag for Egg
GPS - NN 19183 70920

CLIFFS

West
North

Beag for Mor
GPS - NN 19441 71493

Beag for Mercy
GPS - NN 19487 71536

Glen Nevis

Way up

CLIFFS

Col

An Cul Choire

Aonach
Mor

Vallee Verte

CMD Col

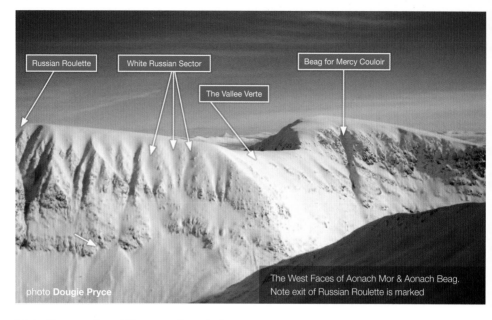

Russian Roulette

White Russian Sector

Beag for Mercy Couloir

The Vallee Verte

The West Faces of Aonach Mor & Aonach Beag.
Note exit of Russian Roulette is marked

photo **Dougie Pryce**

55. Beag for Mercy Couloir

5

similar to:

harder than: Beag for Egg

combine with:

So called because when the author skied this it
was a horrible mix of ice and unstable windslab!
To find the entrance to the Mercy Couloir
climb up the ridge as if going to the summit of
Aonach Beag for about 100metres and then
traverse over the top of the cliffs to your right.
Alternatively you can find the entrance when
skiing off the summit of Aonach Beag by aiming
towards the summit of Carn Mor Dearg (as you
look across this is just to the right of the summit
of Ben Nevis). You can get a reasonably good
look into and down the gully from both sides but
particularly from skier's left. It will often be rocky
at the top and there are a couple of narrow /
steep sections on the way down.

photo **Kenny Biggin**

Looking up Beag for Mercy Couloir after a sketchy
first run

Beag for Mor – Does it get any better?   photo **Kenny Biggin**

Don't switch off yet when you come out of the bottom of the couloir as there is still complicated ground below you – either traverse out right towards the CMD col or pick your way down to the valley floor. The best line is to traverse left and finish up by skiing the 'exit chute' below the Beag for Mor Couloir which also allows you to scope out your next run down!

56. Beag for Mor Couloir

similar to:	Grotto Rush
harder than:	
combine with:	

This is the best line on the West Face of Aonach Beag, and on the right day probably one of the best lines in the book - a really classy narrow twisting couloir which will leave you wanting more! The entrance lies around 20metres skiers left of Beag for Mercy. You can just about see all the way down to check it goes by clambering out a short way along the pinnacle at the entrance on skier's right.

Although there is one fairly narrow and steep section, the gully is usually skiable all the way down – you're unlikely to need a rope but having crampons and axe just in case is a good idea. After leaving the main couloir there is an 'exit chute' lurking below you which makes a memorable end to this classy line.

photo **Kenny Biggin** | rider **Neil Muir**

Sweet turns at the top of Beag for Mor Couloir

photo **Kenny Biggin** | rider **Neil Muir**

Wondering what the future holds, looking down the Beag for Mor Couloir

photo **Kenny Biggin** | rider **Neil Muir**

Opening up at the bottom of Beag for Mor Couloir

Beag for Mor looking spicy!

57. Beag for Egg

similar to:	Bold Rush
harder than:	
combine with:	

Named because this line goes to skier's left of Raw Egg Buttress which hosts a number of climbs. Though still serious, this line is substantially easier and more open than the Mercy or Mor Couloirs and makes a good way to ski off the summit of Aonach Beag into the Vallee Verte. The easiest way to find this line is probably to find the top of Beag for Mor Couloir first and then traverse skier's left along the top of the cliffs for around 500metres – you come to a minor rocky top and then the obvious gully rim opens out.

Alternatively you can ski off the summit of Aonach Beag in a South Westerly direction, roughly towards Sgurr a Mhaim with its attractive looking snow bowl. After just over 600metres of gentle descent the broad ridge ends at a minor top with the gully dropping down an open bay to the right.

Routes out from the West Face of Aonach Beag

There are three main choices:

- Stay high and traverse as high as you can towards the Carn Mor Dearg / Aonach Mor col.
- Ski down to where it flattens out and then skin back to the Carn Mor Dearg / Aonach Mor col. From the col the best bet (providing there is at least some snow) is to follow the Allt Daim as if exiting from the Rush Face and do the walk out to the Quad Chairlift (see Routes out from Rush Face description).
- Follow one of the Vallee Verte routes out into Glen Nevis (see Vallee Verte description).

It is also possible to climb back up to the Aonach Mor / Beag col but this is quite steep and isn't generally very nice ground.

East Face of Aonach Beag

The East Face of Aonach Beag is hidden away and can only really be seen in all its glory from the Grey Corries. Having said that there is a good view of it with binoculars from Roy Bridge and Inverroy if you know where to look and you can also see the Bhealaich Face from the top of Summit Gully. There is some epic riding to be had here and new adventures await! The main face is usually guarded by enormous cornices and getting safe conditions where there is enough snow to ski the entire length of the 600metre face can be tricky.

The East Face of Aonach Beag from Stob a Chul-Choire with the CC Chute in the foreground

photo **Kenny Biggin**

⚠ skimountain

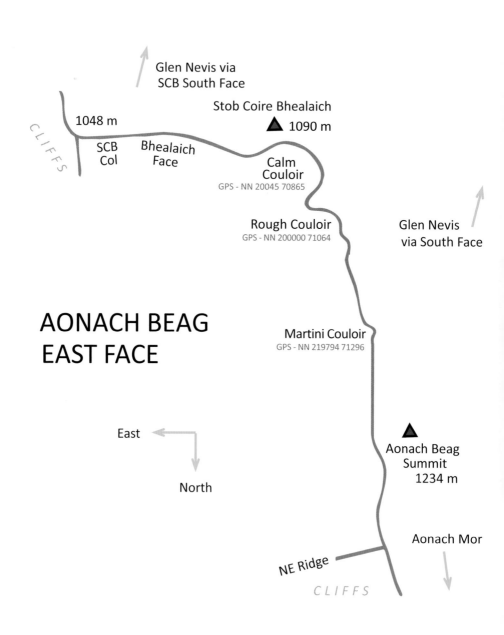

Glen Nevis via
SCB South Face

Stob Coire Bhealaich
▲ 1090 m

1048 m

SCB
Col

Bhealaich
Face

Calm
Couloir
GPS - NN 20045 70865

Rough Couloir
GPS - NN 200000 71064

Glen Nevis
via South Face

CLIFFS

AONACH BEAG
EAST FACE

Martini Couloir
GPS - NN 219794 71296

East

North

▲
Aonach Beag
Summit
1234 m

Aonach Mor

NE Ridge

CLIFFS

Stob Coire Bhealaich

Aonach Beag

Ben Nevis

Martini Couloir

Cul Choire Col

CC Chute

Rough Couloir

Bhealaich Face

Calm Couloir

CB Col

Routes on the East Face of Aonach Beag (from The Grey Corries)

photo **Kenny Biggin**

58. Martini Couloir

		similar to:	
	X	**harder than:**	Hidden Gully
		combine with:	

A steep, long, and gnarly line cutting it's way down the East Face of Aonach Beag. Cornices at the top can be monstrous. Although there is a potential steep line through the cliff band below to exit there will often not be enough snow for this, in which case after skiing the main couloir you need to traverse right to join the lower section of the Rough Couloir.

Author's Note: When I attempted this line I decided I needed to rope in at the top to get past the remnants of some large saggy cornices. I was still on the rope when there was a loud crash and looking across I saw a big solid ice boulder thudding its way down the face – it took a giant bounce before landing lower down on my line and ricocheting off the walls right where I would have been standing ten minutes later. I took that as the mountain telling me to get the hell out of there and let this particular juicy line wait for another day.

photo & rider **Kenny Biggin**

Kenny doing some soul searching at the top of the Martini Couloir

"I was still on the rope when there was a loud crash and looking across I saw a big solid ice boulder thudding its way down the face"

GERMAN ENGINEERED
SINCE 1898

PACKS DESIGNED FOR SNOW & BUILT TO LAST

DEUTERGB.CO.UK

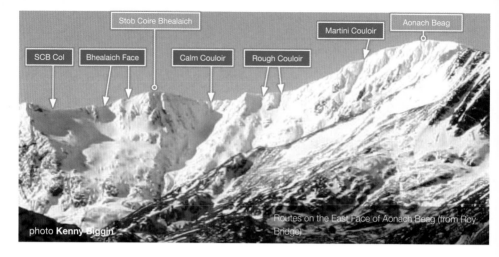

Stob Coire Bhealaich

Aonach Beag

Martini Couloir

SCB Col   Bhealaich Face   Calm Couloir   Rough Couloir

Routes on the East Face of Aonach Beag (from Roy Bridge)

photo **Kenny Biggin**

59. Rough Couloir

similar to:

harder than: Summit Gully

combine with: The Grey Corries

This is a fantastic long couloir taking you down almost 600metres of great skiing into remote backcountry. The name comes from the gaelic for this face which is An Aghaidh Gharbh – The Rough Face. The cornice at the top will often be big and any avalanches coming off the steep East Face above funnel into here so tread carefully. From the summit of Aonach Beag, ski down southwards for around 100metres of height loss keeping the big cornices on your left – this in itself can be a nice ski.

When the gradient eases the entrance is on your left – the best place to look in is usually on a small rise on the right of the entrance. There are a choice of ways in. The top third is reasonably open before everything funnels into a walled gully. After a while things open up again and there is an opportunity to take a rest in a safer spot over to the right.

photo **Neil Muir** | rider **Kenny Biggin**

Below here the gully closes in again for the bottom third and it takes quite a lot of snow to fill this in as there are a couple of steep sections – if you don't fancy staying in the guts of the gully there is easier skiing down the right to the corrie floor.

Looking into the Rough Couloir

60. Calm Couloir

similar to:

harder than:	Rough Couloir

combine with:

The next line along from the Rough Couloir marks the divide between the East Face of Aonach Beag and the start of the Bhealaich Face. This line follows the Allt a Choire Chalma (marked on the 1:25,000 map) and is another stonking run in the right conditions. As with the rest of this area there tend to be big cornices guarding the entry. The Calm Couloir is more serious than the Rough Couloir with a steeper entry and more complications lower down. The easiest entry is usually over on skier's right. After the steep entry, there is a great open central bowl section before it spills into a tighter gully with several significant waterfalls which are tricky to pass except when there is plenty of snow. If there isn't enough snow to get all the way down the bottom section, after the open central section it is easy to escape out to the right with a traverse below the main cliffs of the Bhealaich Face – then you can either pick your way down the left to the bottom or skin out (steeply) to the SCB col.

The entrance to the Calm Couloir waiting for tracks!   photo **Kenny Biggin**

skimountain

Big cornices hanging over the East Face on the summit of Aonach Beag

photo **Kenny Biggin** | rider **Neil Muir**

Spring snow in May on Aonach Beag

photo **Kenny Biggin** | rider **Neil Muir**

photo **Kenny Biggin** | rider

61. Bhealaich Face

4

similar to:

harder than: Chancers

combine with:

There are a variety of lines down the North Face of Stob Coire Bhealaich – these lie in between the two summits marked 1090 and 1048 on the 1:25000 map. You get a great view of this face if you look across from the top of Summit Gully. A line here is a good option if the cornices on the way down the ridge from Aonach Beag have put you off doing anything on the East Face. Essentially the further to skier's right you go the easier it gets, but note that to the East of the second top (marked 1048 on the map) there are some major cliffs which you don't want to go anywhere near.

Skiing a line on this face is a good introduction to skiing on the East of Aonach Beag and will let you get a good look at where the other lines are. After the initial steep section you go across an easier angled slope before arriving at a scattered band of rocks. In lean conditions some good route finding is needed here to pick your way through the rocks with the best way through over towards skier's left of the rock band. It's a long way out from the bottom so a good option can be to skin back up to the SCB Col.

photo **Kenny Biggin** | rider **Neil Muir**

Neil Muir ripping up the Bhealaich Face

 **skimountain**

Skinning up to the SCB Col

photo Kenny Biggin | rider Neil Muir

62. SCB Col

similar to: Yellow Belly

harder than:

combine with:

Really just the right hand variation of the Bhealaich Face but worthy of its own route number since it is substantially easier and more accessible than the rest of the face. Start at the lowest point on the ridge and ski into the open bowl with the rest of the face on your left – the entrance here is similar to Backtrack or Yellow Belly. After the initial steep section you go across an easier angled slope before arriving at a scattered band of rocks. In lean conditions some good route finding is needed here to pick your way through the rocks with the best way through over towards skier's left of the rock band.

Routes out from the East Face of Aonach Beag

Providing there is enough snow the best way out is to ski all the way down to where the angle eases right off before traversing as far left as you can. Then put your skins on and head back up Marians to the col that leads into Summit Gully. You can also skin back up An Cul Choire to the Aonach Mor / Beag col with the impressive North East Ridge on your left. If you've left it late in the season there may not be enough snow for those options and walking round can seem like a long way...

an alternative escape route is to skin back up through the rocks to the SCB col – if you aim for the lowest part on the left (East) it is possible to skin all the way up (depending on snow conditions of course). You could also combine one of these routes with a traverse of the Grey Corries.

Another alternative which may or may not appeal from the bottom is to traverse right and skin / walk up Coire Bhealaich to the low col at Grid Ref: 211706 from where you can get a nice ski (or walk or grass ski) down into Glen Nevis. Keep traversing right if you can and from where you come down to the river it's a 10-20minute walk (or skin) to Steall ruins followed by a half hour walk out through the gorge.

The Grey Corries

Running Eastwards from the Aonachs are the famous Grey Corries. This is a fantastic long ridge of high mountains which have a number of inviting looking bowls. The skiing potential here did not go unnoticed – this was one of a number of potential ski resort locations investigated during the sixties and seventies, and for quite a while was considered by some to be a better option than Nevis Range. Perhaps fortunately, no lifts ever got built here so accessing the great skiing on the Grey Corries remains hard work but very rewarding. There are a number of ways to get onto the ridge, including heading up from Corriechoille near Spean Bridge, or even from Glen Nevis. The best way from this book's offpiste perspective though, is to make use of the lifts!

63. The Grey Corries

combine with: Marians, An Cul Choire

Before you set off, leave a car at the far end of the route on the Corriechoille road at Grid Ref: 256788 - this is just below the edge of the forest at the end of a rough path. This path is actually the remains of the 'puggy line' which was a small railway used to construct the Aluminium Smelter's hydro pipeline that runs underground from Loch Treig to the pipes running down Ben Nevis to the turbines.

Looking East at the Grey Corries from Stob a Chul-Choire

photo **Kenny Biggin** | rider **Kenny Grant**

photo **Kenny Biggin**

Dropping in from Stob Choire Claurigh

photo **Charné Hawkes**

Looking into the freeride bowl in between Stob Coire an Laoigh and Caisteal on the Grey Corries

Start by heading up the Nevis Range lifts and across the summit plateau, then choose a way down into the huge corrie that lies between the Aonachs and the Grey Corries. The easiest ways down here are to ski either Marians or the Cul Choire Col (see the separate descriptions of these routes). Once you are down in the bottom of the corrie your route will depend on how much snow there is – ideally you should do a big long traverse to the right keeping as much height as possible, but there are a number of small gullies etc which will make this tricky unless there is a lot of snow. Pick the line that looks best on the day and ski / skin almost directly East to get to the col named Bealach Coire Easain (Grid Ref: 232722). Heading for this col actually misses out Sgurr Choinnich Beag and Sgurr Choinnich Mor but from a skiing perspective that probably makes sense unless you're feeling purist about doing the 'complete ridge'.

From the col there may be a bit of easy scrambling to get up onto Stob Coire Easain (this will be the trickiest part of the ridge and is normally straight forward). You are now on the main ridge and can start to pick your line down. The route recommended here is to tour all the way along the ridge (probably leaving skins on the whole way) until you get to Stob Choire Claurigh. From the summit here there is a great slanting diagonal line leading down to the North West into the bowl.

Follow the snow down the burn and traverse as far right as you can before aiming for the dam and forest track on the Allt Choimhlidh (Grid Ref: 240765). Be careful not to drop right down into the guts of the main burn leading out of this corrie as it gets quite steep sided and awkward.

From the dam on the Allt Choimhlidh you join a forest track and follow it downhill for around half a kilometre before breaking off onto a rough (and often annoyingly boggy) path on the right (the puggy line) which, after around 2km, will lead you back to the car you left.

The last bit of up at the end of a Grey Corries traverse. The Back Corries and the Ben in the background

photo A helpful hillwalker | rider Kenny Biggin

As you traverse along the ridge there are numerous nice lines dropping into the Northerly bowls – they all ultimately bring you out at the same place and there are routes suitable for all abilities. There are great lines to suit all tastes – from wide open bowls, a couple of steep gully lines, to some short freeride flutes and small cliff drops. Take your pick or if you're feeling fit, ski them all!

There is also plenty of nice skiing to be had dropping off to the South into Glen Nevis, but this leaves you a long way from the road and probably isn't worth it unless you're making a tour of it – perhaps even by including an overnight stay in the Meanach (Luibeilt) or Lairig Leacach bothies.

Ben Nevis

Unfortunately there isn't an accurate statistic to show how many people have sat in pubs talking about skiing the gullies on the North Face of Ben Nevis but never actually even walked up there… however, the numbers may be fairly high. The problem is, talking about it after several beers is relatively easy – getting up there in the right weather, the right snow conditions, with the right people and the right equipment, on the right day, with the right levels of fitness, skill and knowledge, and all before it either gets dark or starts raining, actually turns out to be a pretty big challenge. Hopefully this book will help address some of these issues and the rest will be up to you!

Have Respect

The North Face of Ben Nevis is steeped in mountaineering history and as such skiers and boarders are relative newcomers to the environment… we need to respect climbers and make sure our activities don't either endanger them or detract from their enjoyment of this special place. A group of gung-ho freeride skiers (who've boot packed up the Mountain Track) jumping up and down on top of a massive cornice at the top of Number 2 Gully, smacking the lip with their ski poles, and lobbing ice chunks over the edge 'to see if it slides' is not going to go down well with the five scared climbers on their first winter climbing outing just out of sight halfway down the gully.

photo **Kenny Biggin**

Are you ready? Looking across over Tower Ridge with Number 4 Gully in the middle and Number 5 far right

The Right Snow

Snow conditions on Ben Nevis are tricky to get right – after snow or wind there can be some major avalanches and few safe places to hide so it is not a nice place to be. During much of the winter the North Face and especially the gullies get very little sun so if they aren't full of windslab they will often be too icy (or full of climbers' steps) for an enjoyable ski. Having said that, during the earlier winter months you have more chance of being able to ski from lower down so there can be less walking involved.

Throughout the winter the cornices on the main gullies tend to be huge and can be fairly impassable. At the end of the season the temperatures rise and cornices start to drop off at the same time as the snow starts sagging, creating some impressive crack lines at the tops of the gullies. The rising temperatures release frozen ice and rocks from cliffs above and the risk of full depth and wet snow slides becomes very real.

If you don't mind the walk up to the high snowline, spring conditions from end of April through May and into June are ideal to aim for. Try to get your timing right so that the temperature is cold enough over night to stabilise things but warms up just enough to give you good snow without becoming so warm that everything around you starts to fall off the mountain. Sometimes it is worth aiming to get up top early and then waiting for the snow to be just right before skiing it (and then making a fast retreat before things get any warmer!)

At the end of the season the gullies (in particular Observatory Gully) become littered with rocks that have pinged down from above – wear a helmet and don't loiter for too long!

Access

The skiing on Ben Nevis can be a truly epic adventure but getting up there does a good job of putting most people off. Not only is it Britain's highest mountain at 1344metres, but you have to begin the climb practically from sea level. It should go without saying that it's a trip which you should save for one of the few days where both the weather and the snow are looking good.

The main two access routes are from the North Face car park at Torlundy, or via the Mountain Track from Achintee / Glen Nevis Youth Hostel. Which of these you choose probably depends on how low the snow is and which route you plan to ski down – going up from Torlundy is almost certainly the best option to get you in to the North Face, while the path from Achintee gives you a slight height advantage and a more gentle climb.

Enjoying being on the summit in good vis… for a change!

Mountain Track (Achintee / Glen Nevis)

This is the best option if you plan to go up the 'front' of the mountain. Coming through Fort William from the South, go past the Nevis Bank Hotel, left at the roundabout, then next right before the Inverlochy traffic lights. Then turn right just before the Spar shop in Claggan and follow the single track road to the end. If there is lots of snow you may be able to skin from the car park all the way up the path, though there are usually few (if any) days in a season when this is possible. More common is to be able to skin (fairly steeply) from around the halfway mark where the path crosses the Red Burn – late season you may well be walking all the way to the top! You can also access this path by crossing the bridge opposite the Glen Nevis Youth Hostel which is a more direct (steeper) but slightly lower start. Everyone heading skiing up the Ben should have axe, crampons, map and compass as a minimum.

Timings to the summit from Achintee will vary widely but aiming for 3 or 4 hours will be about right for most depending on fitness, snow conditions, and how much weight you're carrying. Bear in mind that the long standing running record for the Ben Nevis Race is only 1hour 25minutes (up and down, from Claggan park - which is down near the Spar) set in 1984. It would be interesting to see how fast a time could be set on skis with snow cover all the way down – if you take up the challenge start and finish at the Achintee pub and share your time with us on facebook!

North Face Car Park (Allt a Mhuilinn / Torlundy)

Travelling North on the A82, turn right approximately 3 miles after passing the BP garage, go past some buildings and over the railway bridge with traffic lights, then turn immediately right onto a forest track. Keep going for 800m or so until you get to the car park.

From the car park walk another 200m on the flat forest track before turning right onto the North Face path. You will cross the horizontal puggy line path after a couple of minutes - keep going fairly steeply up until you reach a fork. Stay on the main path that leads across to the right (the other path heads steeply up and left to a viewpoint) and keep going until you reach the forest track again. Carry straight on upwards along the track until you get to the upper North Face car park.

This is the point where you will probably realise that some privileged b*****ds have got there before you by driving up the track – this is generally only an option for Forestry or Aluminium Factory employees, Avalanche Forecasters, or for Mountain / Ski Guides who have paid for the key to the gate. Just remind them they are cheating and should be ashamed of themselves (then ask if they'll give you a lift down at the end of the day)!

If you are feeling fit and aren't carrying too much you can get to the upper car park in touring boots in less than half an hour. For many it may well take longer than this!

From the upper car park climb over the stile and you then have two choices – you can either continue up the North Face path which will lead you to the CIC Hut on a good path in around an hour. Or you can cross the burn on your right (the Allt a' Mhuilinn) and head up and right along a rough path that will lead you to the Half Way Lochan (Lochan Meall an t-Suidhe, pronounced Melon Tea). Skirting round the Eastern / left edge of the lochan brings you onto the Achintee Mountain Track and shortly after to where the path crosses the Red Burn (roughly the half way point on the path).

If you opt to continue up the glen to the CIC Hut, there are numerous routes from here up to the top – the easiest is to continue up the side of the burn into Coire Leis and skin steeply up to the col on the right (Grid Ref: 172710). This takes you onto the end of the Carn Mor Dearg Arête and from here you can turn right and skin on up to the summit. This takes you through some steep and fairly exposed ground where you may well need harscheissen, axe and crampons. Another option is to skin / mountaineer up Ledge Route or skin / bootpack up one of the gullies, Number 4 being the easiest.

It always feels good if there is enough snow to start skinning from close to the upper North Face car park but at the end of the season you are more likely to have to walk much further up – commonly well above the CIC Hut or even all the way to the top! On the days when there is only snow high up, having alternative footwear for the walk in (and out) is recommended.

BEN NEVIS

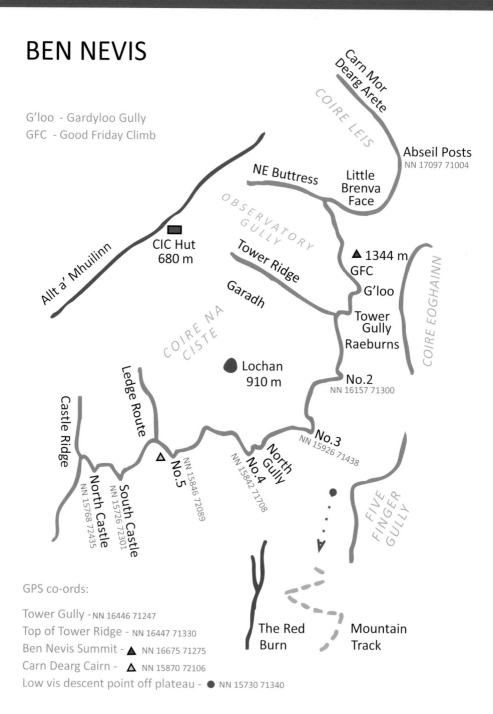

G'loo - Gardyloo Gully
GFC - Good Friday Climb

Carn Mor Dearg Arete

COIRE LEIS

Abseil Posts
NN 17097 71004

NE Buttress

Little Brenva Face

OBSERVATORY GULLY

CIC Hut
680 m

Tower Ridge

▲ 1344 m
GFC

G'loo

Tower Gully

Raeburns

Allt a' Mhuilinn

Garadh

COIRE NA CISTE

COIRE EOGHAINN

Lochan
910 m

No.2
NN 16157 71300

Ledge Route

No.3
NN 15926 71438

Castle Ridge

△ No.5

NN 15846 72089

North Gully
No.4
NN 15842 71708

FIVE FINGER GULLY

North Castle
NN 15768 72435

South Castle
NN 15726 72301

The Red Burn

Mountain Track

GPS co-ords:

Tower Gully - NN 16446 71247
Top of Tower Ridge - NN 16447 71330
Ben Nevis Summit - ▲ NN 16675 71275
Carn Dearg Cairn - △ NN 15870 72106
Low vis descent point off plateau - ● NN 15730 71340

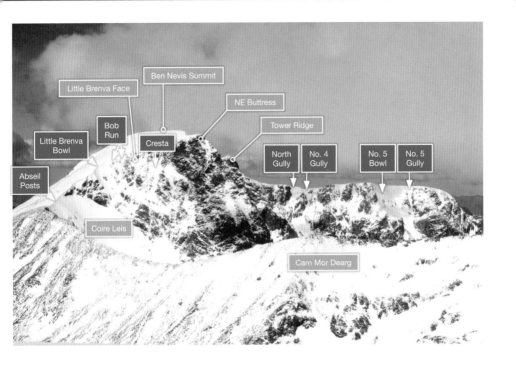

Little Brenva Face

Ben Nevis Summit

NE Buttress

Bob Run

Tower Ridge

Little Brenva Bowl

Cresta

North Gully

No. 4 Gully

No. 5 Bowl

No. 5 Gully

Abseil Posts

Coire Leis

Carn Mor Dearg

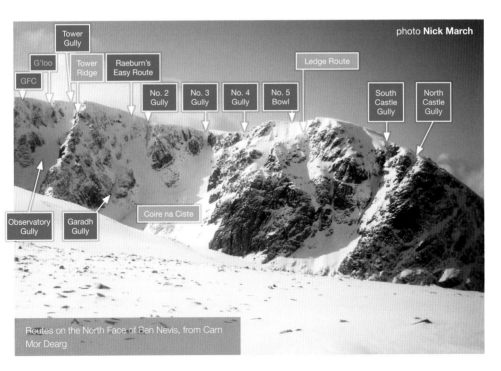

Tower Gully

G'loo

Tower Ridge

Raeburn's Easy Route

Ledge Route

GFC

No. 2 Gully

No. 3 Gully

No. 4 Gully

No. 5 Bowl

South Castle Gully

North Castle Gully

Observatory Gully

Garadh Gully

Coire na Ciste

Routes on the North Face of Ben Nevis, from Carn Mor Dearg

Freeriders setting off from the CIC Hut

CIC Hut

The CIC Hut is the only real alpine hut in
Scotland and has been central to the story of
climbing on Ben Nevis. The hut was built back
in 1928 in memory of Charles Inglis Clark who
was killed in the 1st World War. At 680metres it
provides a fantastic base for some steep skiing
on Ben Nevis though it is more often used by
climbers. The hut doesn't have a guardian or
food, but does have good kitchen facilities,
stoves, gas lighting, and compost toilets.
Sleeping is on bed platforms with comfy foam
mattresses – you will need your own sleeping
bag.

Author's Note: More details on the hut and how
to book places can be found on the Scottish
Mountaineering Club website:
www.smc.org.uk/huts/cic

photo **Kenny Biggin**

Snow lingering late season beside the CIC Hut

© SkiMountain

"And the Pain Shall Set you Free!"

Written by Kenny while helping dig the foundations for the new CIC Hut extension in 2008
John and Danny kept digging most of the summer – Kenny broke after two weeks!

As we trudged up the Allt a Mhuilinn,
On our way to the CIC,
The sun shone bright and the cliff tops laughed,
For what a magical place to be!

The wind was barely a whisper,
While the tranquil burn did chuckle,
And the only sounds to break the spell,
Was the ring of Pick and Shovel.

For they were building an extension,
To house the compost loos,
But in digging the deep foundations,
The boys were paying their dues.

Through mud and rock, topsoil and clay,
And through Glacial Moraine,
The lads were toiling blow by blow,
And the mountains felt their pain.

But Brian McDermott sang and laughed,
And whistled his Irish Melody:
"You're weak boys - I will train you up,
And this will be your Remedy!"

So the guys dug deep and groaned and whimpered,
To build the CIC,
And all the while Brian coaxed them on, chuckling
"The Pain Shall Set you Free!"

 skimountain

Enjoying great snow beside the cairns on the summit plateau on the way to the Red Burn

photo **Ron Cameron** | rider **Bridget Thomas**

64. The Red Burn

similar to:

harder than:

combine with:

The Red Burn (Allt na h-Urchaire) cuts a deep and obvious gash down the front (West) of Ben Nevis on the Glen Nevis side and is the easiest ski to be had on Britain's highest mountain. However, it still has significant steepness to it and in common with routes on the North Face, the Red Burn has also been the site of avalanche fatalities.

Since you can ski this route from the summit of the Ben, potentially all the way down to just above sea level, the Red Burn has to take the prize of the biggest vertical in the British Isles – around 1300metres of vert, at a good angle all the way… what more do you want! More often than not, however, you will be lucky to ski much further than where the tourist path crosses the Red Burn at about half way – still well worth it but in this case you are left with a gruelling trudge both up to and down from the snow line.

In poor visibility take great care with your navigation on the top of Ben Nevis as it is all too easy to get complacent and either walk straight off a North Face cornice, or go the other way into Five Finger Gully – the last place numerous climbers have seen, and the first place the Rescue Team looks. From the large indentation of Garyloo Gully, a 282 degree bearing will take you to the top of the mountain track with the start of the Red Burn just to the right. From the top of Number 4 Gully, heading due West down the fall line will also take you into the top of the Red Burn.

Sometimes a large half-pipe type feature can form in the Red Burn which can form mini cornices so be careful not to fall into this in poor visibility. Continue skiing down until you meet the tourist path at around 700metres at which point you have the choice whether to traverse out to the right along the half-way lochan and across the heather towards the upper North Face car park, or continue down the 'Grassy Bank' and on down the line of the burn or follow the path towards Glen Nevis.

65. North West Face & Carn Dearg Burn

similar to:

harder than: The Red Burn

combine with:

In addition to the Red Burn, there is also an open gully line cutting down the North West Face further to skier's right – this and parts of the face next to it have also been skied but it needs good snow and is a fair bit steeper than the Red Burn. Bear in mind that when a major avalanche released on this burn line a few years ago, the debris spilled well over the Mountain Track almost as far as the lochan – luckily no one was on the path at the time.

The Castle Area

As you look up towards the North Face on the Allt a' Mhuilinn walk in, the first big steep rocky ridge you see is Castle Ridge. Before reaching the main cliffs, there can be some good low level skiing to be had up on the right.

66. Castle Ramp

As you walk from the top North Face car park towards the CIC Hut the first prominent skiable feature you get to is a ramp low down on the ridge on your right. If time is short, you aren't feeling super fit, or if the cloud cover is low, this may be your best option of an interesting ski. This can be a nice alternative to skiing a tight gully and if the snow is low enough it gives two or three hundred metres of great skiing when things higher up are clagged in. As always, beware of avalanche conditions. It is best approached by cutting out to the right towards the halfway lochan. There is even a tight gully line (Castle Ramp Gully) to be explored here.

Aim for around Grid Ref: 154728 and pick a line down from there. A ski here could also be a nice way to finish or extend a ski down the Red Burn.

Castle Gullies

The Castle Gullies are without question two of the classiest gully lines in Scotland and the pair should be on the tick list of any serious Scottish steep skier or boarder. Having said that, they are fairly full on and extremely condition dependent! They are both long, steep, narrow, and avi prone with a tricky exit and the potential to have breaks in them, so they are serious undertakings. Despite being well known, they have probably only been skied a handful of times.

67. South Castle Gully

similar to: Number 2 Gully

harder than:

combine with:

South Castle Gully is on skier's right of 'The Castle' and is perhaps marginally easier than North Castle Gully. This line has particularly impressive towering rock walls on both sides for much of its length. Coming out of the bottom of the main gully the fun is not quite over as you need to get down past a band of cliffs to the floor of the glen. If there is enough snow there is a skiable line through the cliff band directly below, or alternatively traverse out right underneath Carn Dearg Buttress towards Number 5 Gully and go down from there. Do not hang about at the bottom of the gullies or on the traverse out as you are very exposed to avalanches coming from high up above in this area. Both Castle Gullies often have breaks or chockstones in them so have a look at them from near the CIC Hut before dropping in.

68. North Castle Gully

similar to:

harder than:

combine with: South Castle Gully

The steeper (slightly) of the two Castle Gullies, but similar in length and character to the South. The rock walls are not quite as impressive as in the South gully but instead there is a marked camber with the sides constantly closing in on you and sloping across you to the left towards Castle Ridge – this 'slantiness' makes dropping in at the top seem quite bold and the skiing feels pretty intense! This is the lowest full length line on the Ben and as such tends to lose its snow or develop breaks first – the top of North Castle Gully sits at around 1050m – almost 300metres lower than the top of Tower Gully. Once you get to the bottom, why not do the Castle Double and hike back up to tick off South Castle as well?

The Castle Gullies – South Castle Gully on the left photo **Kenny Biggin**

Carn Dearg Summit Gullies

In between the Castle Gullies area and the ridge that forms Ledge Route, and below a minor summit called Carn Dearg, lies a steep hanging snow cirque. There are a couple of gullies here that have seen a ski descent (Arch Gully and Colando Gully), with varying degrees of success. The big problem with the skiing in this bowl is the large cliffs that lie beneath – the corrie is also heavily avalanche prone so very stable conditions are required. The only way to access (or exit from) this part of the Ben is either from the upper part of Ledge Route or by climbing up / abseiling down the winter climbs that lie below such as Harrison's Climb. This area is probably best saved for those with strong skiing and mountaineering skills who have a penchant for exploration and skiing above cliffs.

mountain spirit

HAGLÖFS

OUTSTANDING OUTDOOR EQUIPMENT

Number 5 Gully Area

Beyond the Castle area, the other side of the impressive cliffs that makes up Carn Dearg Buttress, lies one of the biggest gully features on the mountain – Number 5 Gully.

Ledge Route

A great route up the North Face for those with a little mountaineering experience is via Ledge Route. The best variation of this route for ski mountaineers is to start by crossing the burn just below the CIC Hut, cross underneath Number 5 Gully and traverse under some cliffs before cutting up to reach the large snow ledge at mid-height of Moonlight Gully Buttress. From here, cut across Number 5 Gully and then up onto the Ledge Route Ridge. With lots of snow it is possible to skin right from the top North Face car park, up onto the start of the ridge. From there most people will need to change to crampons and axe as there is some easy scrambling involved (though in icy conditions it will be a Grade II winter route and will be much more 'engaging'!). Towards the end of the season (end of May / June) you may get right up to the top of Ledge Route without touching a single patch of snow!

After the short tricky section on Ledge Route, top of Number 5 on the left

photo **Paul Biggin**

En-route to Tower Gully via Ledge Route in June

photo Paul Biggin | rider Kenny Biggin

photo Blair Aitken

Looking across the Moonlight Platform with Ledge Route behind, from the lochan in Coire na Ciste

photo **Blair Aitken** | riders **Paul Easto, Craig Cameron**

Topping out of Number 5 Gully

69. Number 5 Gully

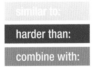

similar to:	
harder than:	Number 4 Gully
combine with:	Ledge Route, Moonlight Gully

After walking past the bottom of the Castle Gullies, this is the first of the big classic gullies that you get to on your way to the CIC Hut. From the hut you get a clear view to the summit although the actual gully proper lies out of sight on viewer's right. The start of Number 5 Gully lies just to skier's right of the cairn at the top of Ledge Route. There are two choices – either ski the gully line or drop into Number 5 Bowl on skier's right. Both are similar gradients though the main gully line is much narrower. Number 5 is usually the first after the Castle Gullies to develop breaks at the end of the season and there can be short narrow, steep and icy sections especially near the middle and towards the bottom depending on conditions. There have been some BIG avalanches here – be warned!

70. Moonlight Gully

similar to:

harder than:

combine with: Number 5 Gully

An exciting and seldom skied variation to skiing the middle reaches of Number 5 Gully is to drop into Moonlight Gully. This is a steep and narrow snow gully taking you down to the large snowy platform cutting across Moonlight Gully Buttress. You can access the top of it by traversing out to skier's right from about a third of the way down Number 5 Bowl. You may well encounter difficulties such as rocks or an ice pitch on the way down so be prepared! From the platform at the end you are best either traversing off to the right, or dropping back into the bottom of Number 5 Gully.

Looking into Coire na Ciste with Number 3, Number 2, Raeburns, and Garadh Gullies clearly visible

photo **Kenny Biggin**

Coire na Ciste

Coire na Ciste is a huge amphitheatre that sits directly above the CIC Hut.

As you're walking up towards the CIC Hut, the best way to access Coire Na Ciste is usually to break out right and cut across the burn before you reach the hut and climb up towards the bottom of Number 5 Gully. Once you're past the initial steepness and about halfway between the CIC Hut and Number 5 Gully, make a gradually upward sloping traverse to your left in the rough direction of Number 3 Gully. This will bring you out at the lochan (which will usually be covered in snow) and from here you can choose which of the gullies (No's 2, 3, or 4) to aim for.

To ski back to the CIC Hut from any of the gullies in this corrie take the left or right bank so that you avoid the band of cliffs that lies in the middle. When the snow is good the best ski is down the right bank, either skirting underneath the Douglas Boulder or dropping into The Chasm but this is only skiable sometimes as especially late season The Chasm loses its snow and becomes a waterfall. Taking the left bank from the lochan is the safer route with easier route finding – keep traversing gently down and left from the lochan until you are roughly underneath Number 5 Gully before descending through the final band of rocks towards the CIC.

71. Tour de la Ciste

similar to:

harder than: Beag and Back

combine with:

If you've walked all the way in to the CIC Hut only to find the summit is all clagged in or you don't fancy any of the gullies, a great low(ish)-level trip is to do a tour of the corrie. This trip will take you over, through, and below plenty of hazards so keep making your own decisions. You can do the tour in either direction or make it up as you see fit but it's a great way to get a really good feel for the place and which of the gullies may or may not be for you. Because the corrie is so huge there is still plenty of skinning and skiing to be had without going all the way to the top.

Start by heading from the CIC Hut to the bottom of Tower Ridge and skirt along the bottom of the Douglas Boulder towards the bottom of Garadh Gully. As you pass round the Douglas Boulder look back to the left to take a look up the Douglas Boulder West Gully – this gully may be a good ski on the right day but it hasn't made it into this book. From here you can also get a really good look up into Garadh Gully.

Instead of heading straight up beside the Garadh here it is usually easier to cut across to your right across the top of The Chasm (the gully / waterfall / terrain trap feature that leads back towards the CIC Hut). Pick your way up between the rocks to get into the main corrie just to the left of where the lochan is. From here kick-turn your way up towards the bottom of Number 2 Gully – before you get there cut out left for a spectacular brew stop on top of the Garadh (the small rocky summit that lies just to skier's left of the top of Garadh Gully). Getting to the top of the Garadh can feel like an achievement in its own right and it's a great viewpoint for the rest of the Corrie. Take a look down into Garadh Gully and up and right to Raeburn's Easy Route.

Either ski steeply down to the base of the Comb from here or traverse across to go higher up into No 2 Gully. You can go a fair way up this slope to get a good ski down. Once you get back towards the lochan you could put your skins back on to take a look into the bottom of No 3, North, and No 4 Gullies. Then on your way back cut along to your left along the snow slope on top of Moonlight Gully Buttress – from here you can see into No 5 Gully, up into Moonlight Gully, and across to Ledge Route. You could finish by skiing the bottom of Number 5 from here or stay on easier slopes on skier's right. Now make your way back to the CIC Hut for a cuppa!

72. Number 4 Gully

similar to:	Easy Gully
harder than:	Chancers
combine with:	Red Burn, Abseil Posts

Number 4 Gully is the easiest of the main North Face gullies and provides the best option for those new to skiing the steeps of Ben Nevis. It should not be taken lightly though as cornices can be

Looking down Number 4 Gully   photo **Katie Fleming** | rider **Neil Fleming**

massive and of course big avalanches are not uncommon. There is a cairn with a metal '4' on it at its entrance but remember this could easily be buried in deep snow so should not be relied on for navigation. The gully starts with a reasonably wide entrance onto a fairly steep but short scarp slope followed by a relatively gentler gradient. The gully then takes a dogleg to the right through a narrower and steeper section before opening out into the wide open expanse of Coire na Ciste. Number 4 Gully is also one of the more accessible routes to climb up (at Grade I) and combining it with either the Red Burn or the Coire Leis Abseil Posts makes a great round trip and is a brilliant way of familiarising yourself with where everything is and the general scale of the Ben.

photo **Kenny Biggin**

Tourists at the top of Number 4 Gully making it look steeper than it is!

photo Katie Fleming | rider **Neil Fleming**

Bootpacking up Number 4 Gully

photo **Kenny Biggin**

Number 4 Gully cairn

73. North Gully

similar to:

harder than: Number 3 Gully

combine with:

Directly alongside Number 4 Gully (to skier's right) is North Gully which from a distance looks like a fantastic ski. The main problem with North Gully is that the normal exit to it is often more of an ice pitch which you may have to abseil or downclimb. Best to take a good look from the bottom first, perhaps by climbing up it.

Number 4 Gully on the right with North Gully looking spicier on the left

photo **Kenny Biggin**

74. Number 3 Gully

similar to:

harder than: Number 4 Gully

combine with:

Number 3 Gully sits smack in the middle of the corrie and is the most obvious gully feature when looking up from the CIC Hut. It is relatively short compared to other gullies on the Ben but is still plenty steep and long enough to get scared in! The entrance at the top is by far the trickiest part and can be frighteningly steep. After the entrance, Number 3 is relatively open and you get a great ski down the centre of the corrie towards the lochan.

Reaching the cornice at the top of Number 2 Gully   photo Blair Aitken | rider Craig Cameron

75. Number 2 Gully

similar to:	Hidden Gully
harder than:	Number 3 Gully
combine with:	

Number 2 Gully is a long, narrow, and steep couloir which is harder and more serious than Number 3 (though the entrances can be similar). There can be an ice pitch in it and the cornice at the top can be massive. Gav MacKay and Ben Thorburn skied it 'free' from the top in 1996 and it was also skied from the top on telemarks by Al Reid and Ally Coull in 2001. It now sees descents most seasons but is still a full on gully with a cornice and scarp slope more than capable of putting anyone off when it's not in condition. It is usually wide enough to fit skis in the whole way down, but only just in places!

photo **Al Reid** | rider **Ally Coull**

Ally Coull dropping into Number 2 from the top on teles in 2001

Al Reid in amongst it in Number 2 on teles in 2001

76. Garadh Gully

similar to:

harder than:

combine with:

It's almost impossible to give an accurate description of this gully as it can change so dramatically. It has had very few ski descents and will never be anything other than steep and committing but it will also regularly be pretty unskiable! Make sure you have a very good look at it from below before committing at the top (the top is a convex roll over so you can't see down until you're in it). The main feature to worry about is an ice pitch that sits near the bottom of the gully – in lean years this pitch isn't skiable while in a bumper year it fills right in.

77. Raeburn's Easy Route

similar to:

harder than:

combine with:

One of the few routes in this book that fits solidly into the 'Le Ski Extreme' category. Bear in mind that the 'Easy' in the title is from a climber's perspective, not a skier's. The route lies up and to skier's right of Number 2 Gully and is usually classed as a Grade II/III winter climb. It is a big steep face route which is exposed for its entirety over cliffs. To exit the face down into Coire na Ciste a 30metre abseil is required. Good luck!

Author's Note: To give you a little insight before trying this one, here are some selected quotes from Steve Wilcox's description of skiing this route in April 2009:

"...hard and icy on the main face... 60 degree slope... skis sounded like fingernails running down a chalk board.... the traverse section was the most tricky with a change of fall-line, a big mogul bump then a sharp left hand turn... I only just managed to stop in time for the 30m cliff by slapping my right ski on an exposed rock... And then the rockfall from above started!" Mmm... you're selling it to us Steve!

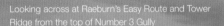

Looking across at Raeburn's Easy Route and Tower Ridge from the top of Number 3 Gully

photo **Kenny Biggin**

Looking up to Garadh Gully with The Chasm
dropping out of sight below

Observatory Gully Area

Beyond Coire na Ciste and the CIC Hut, two giant ridges dominate the North Face – these are Tower Ridge and North East Buttress. In between these two great ridges lies the Observatory Gully area.

78. Observatory Gully

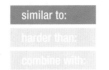

similar to:	Tour de la Ciste
harder than:	
combine with:	

For those who reckon Tower Gully from the top is a bit too much for them, there is a great (but not too serious) ski to be had in epic surroundings by skinning / bootpacking up from the bottom of Tower Ridge into Observatory Gully and then skiing back down from the level of the top of Tower Scoop (the cliff band which sits underneath the top pitch of Tower Gully). The skiing from here is open and not too steep by this point and the setting of this place is probably unequalled anywhere in Britain – with mountaineering history all around you: Gardyloo Gully directly above, Tower Ridge and Echo Wall to skier's left, and North East Buttress and a raft of classic climbs on the giant cliffs on skier's right – including Indicator Wall, Point Five and Zero Gullies, the Minus and Orion Faces, and Observatory Ridge. Be aware that rockfall (and cornice collapse) from above is a major hazard in here as especially in warm weather missiles can land with alarming precision right where you plan to ski – wear a helmet!

Looking up Observatory Gully – left to right: Observatory Buttress with Good Friday Climb above, Gardyloo Gully with obvious break at the chockstone, Tower Gully showing the dogleg above Tower Scoop, Tower Ridge on the right

One last glance at the Tower Gully entrance before getting the skis on!

79. Tower Gully

similar to:	
harder than:	Number 5 Gully
combine with:	Ledge Route, Tower Ridge, Triple Crown

Probably one of the best known ski descents in Scotland, Tower Gully has got to be one of the all-time classics. The start of the gully is only 200metres away from the summit and at the same height. For much of the season there tend to be very big cornices making dropping in from the top tricky if not impossible. Later in the season (e.g. in May or often into June), the cornice difficulties lessen and in good spring snow the gully starts to see lots of descents with many hardened ski mountaineers making the pilgrimage to ski Tower Gully as a great way to end their season. Although it is reasonably open at the top, it is still respectably steep and the top section should be seen as a no-fall zone since it lies directly above the cliffs at Tower Scoop (no pressure!). Normally there is a dog-leg to the left after the top pitch and then you head right to traverse along the top of Tower Scoop to take you over into the less stressful open environment of Observatory Gully. Note that it can be icy between the Scoop and Gardyloo since there is less sun here.

In 2013, Peter MacKenzie and Al Todd set up a real classic (though fairly hard) ski mountaineering prize by combining Tower Gully with an ascent of Tower Ridge for the 'Tower Double'. A more reasonable objective requiring less mountaineering skill is to access Tower Ridge via Ledge Route, or combine Tower Gully with a scoot over Carn Mor Dearg and Aonach Mor to tick off the Triple Crown.

Not a landing you want to mess up – Peter MacKenzie dropping into Tower Gully from the top after coming up Tower Ridge with Al Todd

photo **Al Todd** | rider **Peter MacKenzie**

Savouring the last steep snow of the 2013 season at the top of Tower Gully

photo **Paul Biggin** | rider **Kenny Biggin**

⚠ skimountain

80. Gardyloo Gully

There have been several attempts at skiing Gardyloo Gully with varying degrees of success (or failure). The gully is very steep and usually has a large chockstone boulder blocking the way near the top – in lean snow a squeeze tunnel leads under this and in a real bumper snow year it can get covered. There is often an ice pitch both above and below the chockstone.

Author's note: At the time of writing no information was available about a complete ski descent of Gardyloo, though there is an unconfirmed rumour that it has been skied successfully. It has definitely been skied from around 30metres under the chockstone and also fallen down from beside the chockstone following a binding failure!

81. Good Friday Climb

You can always trust the French to set the bar unreasonably high. Back in February 1982, the Chamonix guide Jean Franck Charlet came across and did just that by skiing Good Friday Climb. His descent was a 'trial run' for a live BBC documentary instigated by mountaineering legend Hamish MacInnes – the actual live broadcast had to be cancelled at the last minute due to horrendous weather. The Ben was plastered in snow at the time but even then Jean Franck had to do two short abseils (on pre-fixed ropes) to get past two small ice falls.

It is well worth reading Hamish MacInnes's account of this episode in his book *Beyond the Ranges* – there were multiple helicopters, several tons of expensive camera equipment, a platoon of marines camped on the summit, extreme storm conditions and a number of (unrelated) fatalities in the mountains at the same time.

The line drops steeply down the North Face just beyond the summit cairn and is on the skier's right of Indicator Wall (the cliffs to skier's right of Gardyloo Gully). It is usually a Grade III winter climb. If you manage to successfully negotiate the first 200metres a large snow terrace takes you back above cliffs into Observatory Gully at the bottom of Gardyloo Gully.

Jean Franck Charlet dropping into Good Friday Climb in 1982

photo **Jean Franck Charlet collection**
rider **Jean Franck Charlet**

Jean Franck making that all important first turn in Good Friday Climb

Jean Franck checking it's not too steep to ski

Looking down Good Friday Climb

Mountain TV epic is a washout

THE great Ben Nevis TV spectacular became a triple washout yesterday. The climb which was to have taken three men and a woman to the 4,406-feet summit was called off because of atrocious weather.

It had been postponed from Saturday. And the daring ski descent by Frenchman Jean Charlet also fell victim to the torrential rain and dense cloud.

The happiest person in Fort William yesterday was his wife Sylvane, 29. She said: "Jean will be safe today."

Jean, 29, wasn't so pleased. His test run through lethal boulders last week lasted 15 minutes and was described as brilliant.

The climb, master-minded by producer Mike Begg, who, with Scot Hamish McInnes involved 60 BBC personnel, 15 Royal Marines, two tons of television equipment, the constant use of two helicopters and an estimated cost of around £100,000.

It would have been the first live TV broadcast of a winter climb on the mountain's fearsome north-east face. It is now hoped to record it if the weather improves.

Hamish, 51, was slightly hurt at the weekend when a falling boulder gashed his head. His girl-friend Betsy Brantley, 26, is in the climbing team.

A reminder of how great skiing deeds got reported prior to Facebook

JEAN and **SYLVANE** . . she's happy he's not going downhill

Coire Leis

Coire Leis sits at the far end of the North Face well beyond the CIC Hut.

82. Abseil Posts

 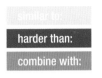

similar to:	
harder than:	Yellow Belly
combine with:	The Red Burn or Number 4 Gully

Along with the Red Burn, this is one of the easiest routes to ski on the Ben. It makes a great ski from the summit but only in good visibility and not when it's icy as there are some nasty convex rollovers in both directions as you ski off the plateau. From the summit it's worth sliding gently out along the ridge to the East where you can get a great view of the North Face from the top of North East Buttress. After taking some photos from here, carefully traverse back across to skier's right until you're well away from the steep edge of the Little Brenva Face and then ski down around 200metres in a South Easterly direction to a large flat area which marks the Western end of the Carn Mor Dearg Arete. There are a number of entrances from here into Coire Leis which are similar to dropping into Coire Dubh at Nevis Range. Note that the actual abseil posts were removed in 2012, but the name sticks.

photo **Kenny Biggin**

Sweet tracks down the Abseil Posts line in Coire Leis

83. Little Brenva Bowl

Further up Coire Leis from the Abseil Posts route there is a much steeper line cutting through the cliffs on skier's right of the Little Brenva Face (in between the climber's lines Bob Run and the Final Buttress). The feasibility of the line here is snow dependent and it's worth getting a good look on the way up to check there isn't an ice pitch lurking near the bottom before dropping in. If the Little Brenva Bowl isn't exciting enough for you, the line of Bob Run which lies to the left of some rocks has also been skied. A steep line down a hanging couloir in the middle of the face further to skier's left known as Cresta has also seen a partial ski descent (by Martin Burrows-Smith) from below the summit rocks.

84. Coire Eoghainn

On the Southern aspect of Ben Nevis in between the summit and the top of the Abseil Posts route, there are a couple of possible lines that have been skied down into Glen Nevis. The slope leading from the summit almost directly South is arguably the longest continuous steep slope in Scotland.

Martin Burrows-Smith recalls having a magnificent run here all the way down to the top Glen Nevis car park with great snow all the way in the mid-eighties. Jimmy Ness also has some excellent tales of skiing on this side of the mountain in the great snow they used to get all the way back in the mid-forties and fifties. On one occasion Jimmy was camping on the summit and heard Jimmy Marshall (the famous climber) and his brother trying to dig unsuccessfully down to the Observatory which was well burried under the snow. Since it was such freezing temperatures, Jimmy took pity on the climbers and allowed them into his tent on the condition that they would help him massage the frostbite out of his feet. Next time you're complaining about your equipment or about not having light enough kit, just think of the weight of the gear these guys used to lug up there.

These days, the snow is rarely deep and low enough on this Southerly aspect to make Coire Eoghainn seem worthy of many descents. If you do decide to venture this way, beware of the various steep hazards - in particular The Great Waterslide (Allt Coire Eoghainn) should be treated with great caution. It is also possible to drop down toward Meall Cumhann or the Vallee Verte but again lack of snow is likely to be an issue here, although an enticing gully lies waiting for a descent here in the right conditions.

corvus
skis by black crows

Stob Ban

Sitting in the shadow of Ben Nevis and only one of the long chain of mountains that makes up the Mamores, Stob Ban still deserves its own mention within this book because of some classic gullies that cut down through the North East face. Both routes described here are approached by parking at the Lower Falls car park in Glen Nevis (at 100metres, Grid Ref: 145683) and skinning (or walking) along the line of a good path that leads up the left (East) bank of the Allt Coire a' Mhusgain. You get onto the path by crossing over a stile close to the Lower Falls marked Mamore Grazings. Go through the gate in the deer fence and continue up the East bank. After around half an hour you come

Bootpacking up South Gully on Stob Ban

to a second gate in a deer fence and a flattish area. After this, the burn goes through a gorge and the best line to skin usually takes you further up and out to the left to avoid skinning along the steep bank.

Once the gorge finishes you can see up to your right into the main cliffs and gullies from the corrie. As you look up at the cliffs, South Gully lies to the left with North Gully (hidden until you get fairly close) to the right. There are actually more gullies hidden away on Stob Ban and some classic descents to be had by going left onto Sgurr a Mhaim, so keep your eyes peeled if you fancy exploring!

Yet another classic Scottish gully descent that rarely gets skied! South Gully on Stob Ban

Dropping into North Gully, Stob Ban

85. SB South Gully

This is a classy and fairly accessible gully and a great objective for a more interesting ski tour if the snow is reasonably low. The line is the most obvious seen from the skin in and the simplest thing to do is bootpack up the gully and ski back down, although you could of course make more of a loop and keep your skins on for longer by going up Stob Ban's East ridge. South Gully can be reasonably steep at the very top, but not for long and in general the angle is fairly forgiving in good snow. There are impressive rock walls and great views down into the glen making for a pretty cool day out!

86. SB North Gully

similar to:	Easy Gully
harder than:	South Gully

Just beyond the summit of Stob Ban lies North Gully which has a similar feel to South Gully but is definitely a little steeper, especially at the entrance. The gully starts off wide and open before squeezing together between rock walls without ever getting too narrow. Another great day out and even better in combination with South Gully!

Selected Local Tours

Although this is more of an offpiste guidebook than a ski touring one, there is of course plenty of crossover. There are so many potential outings to be had in this area that the touring deserves at least a mention. The following section gives a brief overview of a small selection of the more obvious (or interesting) ski tours in the area close to Nevis Range and Ben Nevis. There are many others but they can wait for a future book.

87. Chno Dearg

starting height	Fersit - 240m / Corrour – 400m
summit height	1046m
start	Fersit or Corrour

You can either do a loop over this munro and its neighbours from Fersit or from Corrour train station. If you opt to get an early train out to Corrour it whisks you up to 400metres, giving you a nice leg up to where the snow is. There are a number of fantastic routes you can access from Corrour but heading along a flat start to the long sloping ridge that takes you up onto Meall Garbh (976metres) is probably one of the best outings. There is some gully exploration to be done here for those with enough left in their legs. From the top of Meall Garbh there is a gentle ski over onto Chno Dearg followed by a great 800metre descent down to Fersit.

The alternative is to do a loop from the car park at Fersit - the Chno Dearg Horseshoe. The turn-off to Fersit is several miles East of Roy Bridge on the A86. Park at the end of the public road where there is a small car park (Grid Ref: NN345781) with a right of way marker pointing to Steisean Choire Odhair and Corrour Station. Start by heading down and across the bridge and then along the track that leads through the farm, then roughly follow the Allt Chaorach Beag up towards the lochan and strike out onto the North ridge leading to the summit of Stob Coire Sgriodain at 979metres. From here there are a number of good descents or continue round the horseshoe onto Meall Garbh and then Chno Dearg before returning to Fersit.

Author's Note: Another nice mountain close by if you want to explore is Stob a Choire Mheadhoin – park at Grid Ref: NN349789 where there is a millstone that dates way back to the fifteenth century. This belonged to Angus of Fersit, 2nd Chief of Keppoch – there isn't any photographic proof but perhaps Angus was one of the first Highland freeriders!

88. Stob Choire Claurigh

starting height	200m
summit height	1177m
start	Corriechoille

The Grey Corries have already featured earlier in the book as a route you can ski from the lifts at Nevis Range. However, these hills are also a good option for a self propelled trip with a reasonably high starting point. Although it is a private road, it is normally possible to drive up to the old puggy line just before the forest and park here (Grid Ref: NN256788). The most obvious and direct route is to follow the forest track up through the gate and past The Wee Minister until you come out of the trees (Grid Ref: NN262776) and then break out onto the broad North ridge. In good snow this is a nice ridge to skin up but it does have a tendency to get scoured so can be hard work until around 800metres where it starts to open out and give you a better view of where you're going.

There are several alternative ways up – one option is to continue up the Lairig Leacach glen and approach via one of the many bowls and ridges on offer here. For an expedition with a rather long start, you could even go all the way through to the Lairig Leacach bothy and either follow the Allt a Chuil Choirean or do a tour over Stob Ban to approach Stob Choire Claurigh from the South. You can also start by walking South West from your car along the puggy line, then follow the Allt Choimhlidh in order to gain access to the good skinning on offer in the North Western bowls.

Once on top of Stob Choire Claurigh there are a range of good skiing options. Obviously one option is to tour back along the main Grey Corries ridge until you find a descent you like the look of. Or head East along the scrambly ridge that leads to Stob Coire na Ceannain. There is some nice skiing on offer in these Eastern most bowls and faces of the Grey Corries. You can get a good look into this area to pick your line in advance with binoculars from Roy Bridge and Inverroy.

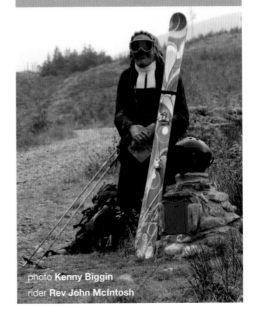

The Wee Minister – "Good fortune to all who pass this way"

photo **Kenny Biggin**
rider **Rev John McIntosh**

So who brought my skis? Woof! On Stob Choire Claurigh

photo **Ron Cameron** | rider **Paul Biggin and Roy**

89. Beinn Teallach

starting height	270m (use OS Sheet 34)
summit height	915m
start	Roughburn

Soon after passing the Laggan Dam as you're heading East on the A86, you cross a rocky burn with parking on the left at Roughburn (Grid Ref: NN377813). From here follow the forest track through the gate and after half a kilometre branch left to come out of the forest. Follow the Allt a' Chaorainn for another kilometre before breaking out up the broad ridge that leads along to the summit of Beinn Teallach. From here you can either return the way you came, do a tour further into the backcountry to end up returning over Beinn a' Chaorainn, or drop down more steeply on the East face (which is a good ski but can leave a fairly long slog out if the snow isn't ideal).

If there is plenty of snow, there is also a good alternative day out on generally gentle West facing slopes if you approach Beinn Teallach from Glen Roy. Turn off the A86 in Roy Bridge to Bohenie and follow the Glas Dhoire glen until the forest opens out onto the open bowls of Beinn Teallach's West Face.

© SkiMountain

90. Beinn a' Chaorainn

starting height	270m (use OS Sheet 34)
summit height	1049m
start	Allt na h-Uamha or Roughburn

Two kilometres further East on the A86 from the parking for Beinn Teallach, there is a small bridge over a burn with a parking bay on the right (South) of the road (Grid Ref: NN401819). This is the most direct starting point to approach Beinn a' Chaorainn from but the path can be extremely muddy due to the popularity of this burn for canyoning. You may prefer the less muddy but longer start along forest tracks from Roughburn. Either way, the most obvious route is to strike up the broad South ridge to get to the summit. Alternatively, you can follow the Allt na h-Uamha up the glen and either keep going up to the Bealach a' Bharnish or for more of a ski mountaineering expedition try the East ridge (Grid Ref: NN392851) which takes you directly to the summit. Once on the summit there are some fantastic skiing options here – the choice, as they say, is yours...

There is also a plethora of skiing on offer just further East on Creag Meagaidh but that deserves its own section in a future Cairngorms book.

91. Scottish Haute Route

timings	7 or 8 days
distance / Height	160km / 10,000m ascent
start	Fort William or Ballater

This is a long but enticing challenge that as far as is known has only been completed twice – once by David Grieve and Mike Taylor (with Sandy Cousins and Derek Pyper to Dalwhinnie) in 1978, then by Roger and Finlay Wild in 2010. Both parties took slightly different routes and went in opposite directions, but the concept was the same – a high level traverse across Scotland on skis, linking together some of the biggest and best mountains. Both expeditions were written up in the SMC Journal and these are well worth getting hold of if you are thinking of an attempt – David Grieve's article was in Vol. XXXI, 1978, No. 169, while Roger Wild's article was in Vol. XL1, 2010, No. 201.

In essence the Scottish Haute Route links Fort William in the West with Ballater in the East. This joins together the two highest mountain ranges in Scotland and incorporates Ben Nevis, Carn Mor Dearg, the Aonachs, The Grey Corries, Ben Alder, Cairn Toul, Ben MacDui, Beinn a' Bhuird, and Ben Avon amongst others. The route seems to split fairly well into a week long tour with a good selection of overnight options. The likely candidates for accommodation include a choice of bothies: Lairig Leacach, Staoineag, Ben Alder Cottage, Culra, Ruigh-aiteachan, and the Hutchison Hut. That both parties were able to use a slightly different selection of sleeping quarters shows how lucky we are to have the bothy network. Both groups placed strategic food caches in advance and had an overnight stop in Dalwhinnie. An overnight 'approach stop' was also made in both cases to start the trip off – on the summit of Ben Nevis in the West and Carndavon Lodge in the East.

It goes without saying that an attempt is only really an option during the fairly rare windows of time when the snow and weather plays ball, but with luck perhaps it will be a little less than 32 years before the next successful traverse is completed.

Heavy bags on the Scottish Haute Route – Sgurr Choinnich Mor behind

photo Roger Wild | rider Finlay Wild

Heading East on the Grey Corries at the start of the Scottish Haute Route

photo **Finlay Wild** | rider **Roger Wild**

Go Exploring

Do not feel constrained to touring on the small selection of routes given here – the access laws in Scotland give you the right to responsible access almost everywhere so the main limit to where you seek adventure is your imagination. There are many excellent ski touring possibilities in this area so do not neglect mountains such as The Mamores (especially Mullach nan Coirean and Sgurr a' Mhaim), Beinn Bhan, Meall na Teanga, Gulvain, the Ben Alder and Laggan hills, the Knoydart hills, and others which have all felt the occasional slide of P-tex on their slopes. Go exploring - the mountains await!

High Roads

Since it is quite rare for there to be good snow cover down to sea level, the routes that see touring traffic most often tend to be the ones with high roads passing beneath. Here is a table with a small selection of roads and heights that may be of interest for those planning ski tours. Not all of these locations are good starting points to tour from but it may help fuel your imagination for route finding.

Local High Roads	Height
Glen Loy	110m
Glen Nevis	150m
Lundavra	180m
Corriechoille	200m
Glen Gloy	200m
Aviemore	210m
Glen Roy	220m
Fersit	240m
Loch Cluanie	240m
Loch Laggan	280m
A87 Loch Garry	350m
A889 to Dalwhinnie	350m
Glensherra	350m
Fechlin	350m
Corrour Train	400m

Local Bothies and Huts

Also of interest to ski tourers may be huts and bothies. The CIC on Ben Nevis is the only proper mountain hut (see Ben Nevis section) but there is also Loch Ossian Youth Hostel close by Corrour train station which at the time of writing has reduced but still reasonable opening during winter. Bothies are very basic but have the benefit of being open and free – don't expect there to be anything left in these shelters so you will need to carry everything required to sleep and eat including food, stove, fuel, pan, sleeping bag & matt, etc. Many though not all of the bothies are maintained by volunteers working with the Mountain Bothies Association charity.

For more details, see:

- CIC Hut - www.smc.org.uk/huts/cic
- Loch Ossian Youth Hostel - www.syha.org.uk
- Mountain Bothies Association - www.mountainbothies.org.uk

Name	Height	Grid Ref
CIC Hut (book via SMC)	680m	NN167722
Lairig Leacach	470m	NN282736
Staoineag	300m	NN296678
Meanach (Luibealt)	340m	NN266685
Loch Ossian Youth Hostel	390m	NN371670
Luib Chonnal (Glen Roy)	330m	NN394936
Culra (Ben Alder)	470m	NN523762
Ben Alder Cottage (haunted!)	360m	NN499680
Glensulaig (Fassfern)	170m	NN030833
Gleann Dubh-lighe	80m	NM944819
Corryhully (Glenfinnan)	60m	NM912844
Invermallie	50m	NN136888
A'Chuil	100m	NM944924
Sourlies	10m	NM869950
Barisdale (small fee/night)	10m	NG872048
Glenpean	80m	NM936903
Kinbreak	190m	NN002961

A Potted History

Unlike climbing there has not been a strong history of recording routes skied and first descents in Scotland. For this reason it is impossible to write an accurate account of who skied what and when – many ground breaking first descents will have been done quietly amongst friends, or even solo, and quickly lost in the mists of time. There will also be routes which have multiple skiers or groups out there who believe they made the first descent… who would want to break that illusion? It is one of the downsides of publishing this guide that future skiers will no longer easily feel like they are breaking new ground (though there are still new lines to be spotted if you look closely); the flipside is that future skiers will find it much easier to find and repeat existing routes.

Having said that the history is hazy, and at the risk (or certainty) of missing people out, the following section gives a quick overview of a few selected nuggets of historical background to skiing in this area.

Ben Nevis – Formative Years

The Scottish Mountaineering Club (SMC) have records of skiing on Ben Nevis dating back as early as 1904, with The Red Burn being skied by William Naismith and Allan Arthur in 1909. After that, we need to skip through to after the 2nd World War when there was some ex-army kit sloshing around and a number of separate groups including the likes of Jimmy Ness and Bobby Corson are known to have skied on Ben Nevis and elsewhere during the mid to late forties and fifties.

photo **Jimmy Ness**
riders **Donnie MacPherson, Jimmy Ness, Jimmy Wynne**

photo **Jimmy Ness**
rider **Donnie MacPherson**

Back when skis were skis and men were men – Ben Nevis, circa 1950

© SkiMountain

The late fifties and sixties saw skiing become a mass participation activity with many people heading for the new ski resorts in Glencoe, Aviemore, and Glenshee. Despite the attraction of the lifts there were still a good number of activists ski touring around the Fort William area, including Audrey and Douglas Scott and others during the sixties and seventies. By the late seventies there were some great ski touring objectives being ticked off, such as David Grieve, Mike Taylor and others skiing the Lochaber 4000ers in 1977 and then the Scottish Haute Route in '78, which wasn't repeated until Roger and Finlay Wild took up the challenge during 2010.

During the seventies the extreme skiing revolution was well underway in the Alps with a huge number of audacious new routes being skied – some of which have yet to be repeated. Steep skiing took a while to take hold in Scotland but during the 1980's things took off with a bang with Jean Franck Charlet skiing Good Friday Climb on Ben Nevis in 1982 and Martin Burrows-Smith collecting an impressive list of the Ben Nevis gullies including all the main gullies (Tower and Numbers 3, 4, and 5 from the top, and Number 2 from below the cornice). Martin also ticked off some of the harder lines in this era including both Castle Gullies, Garadh Gully, Moonlight Gully, plus explorations of Bob Run and Cresta on the Little Brenva Face.

The Rise of Nevis Range

Alongside the development of extensive lift systems in the Alps and improvements in ski and binding designs, Alpine skiing continued to gain in popularity through the fifties and the first fixed ski lift was built at Glencoe in 1956 followed shortly after by a T-bar at Glenshee in 1957 and a chairlift at Cairngorm in 1961.

Skiing became hugely popular during the sixties, and the early resorts became so busy that sites for new developments were investigated with some of the main candidates being at Creag Meagaidh, The Grey Corries, Dalwhinnie Corries, Drumochter, Ben Wyvis, and Aonach Mor. A preliminary survey of all these sites was completed (by Eric Langmuir and Bob Clyde) but plans were largely put on the back burner.

The first major post-war depression hit Britain in 1973, hitting the High Street hard, and by the end of the decade bad news was the last thing Fort William needed. However, the Pulp Mill closure in 1980 along with modernisation of the aluminium smelter resulted in huge job losses. These drastic events left Fort William looking for ways to revitalise itself and in parallel the idea of turning Fort William into a ski resort was being dusted off. When Ian Sykes and Ian Sutherland (Spike and Sudsy, who started Nevisport in 1970) hiked up and managed to score an epic trip all the way down Aonach Mor in great snow, they started to pursue the idea in earnest.

Spike had an exploratory meeting with the Highlands and Islands Development Board and afterwards it took only a week for local businesses (led by Nevisport and local hotel owner Ian Milton) to raise the £1million required to call the Development Board's bluff and ask them to start talking seriously about getting the project off the ground.

In the years leading up to the lifts being built, Spike and Sudsy and a number of others were active in hiking up Aonach Mor to suss out what the skiing on offer was really like and where it might make sense to place lifts and snow fences. The pre-lift years were also the pinnacle of the diminutive Lochaber heli-skiing era – one day in 1988 Spike and Ed Grindley used a chopper to ski the two main bowls of Carn Mor Dearg, Summit Gully, The Red Burn, and Number 4 Gully. Myrtle Simpson, Mike Jardine, Keith Geddes and others had several more heli-excursions around this time and during these initial forays, most of the well known lines in the main Back Corries area got skied - Spike's Fright, Summit Gully, Coire Dubh, the Nid Ridge, and even the Sgurr Finnisg-aig slopes all got skied.

On another crucial day in Nevis Range's history, a chopper lifted 200 people including politicians, financiers, and media, along with five rope tows, up to the top of the Goose on Aonach Mor – thankfully they got lucky and had great conditions for this event which could have backfired if the snow and weather gods had been in a bad mood.

The definition of 'a jolly'. Scoping out the Back Corries before the lifts were built

photo **Nevis Range Collection**

riders **Spike, Rory Simpson, Tinker Fraser, Mike Jardine, Bill Dale, Craig McGeoghie, Jim Gunn, Gordon Fraser**

photo Ian Sykes Collection
Nevis Range Top Station under construction

photo Ian Sykes Collection
rider Willie Anderson

Man in hole

photo Ian Sutherland
riders Ian Sykes, Ron Gretton, Gerald McIntyre

Working out where the lifts should go

After almost ten years of heartache, hard work, and political battles, they finally succeeded in getting the project off the ground. The end of the eighties saw work begin on the ski lifts at Nevis Range and the newest Scottish ski resort finally opened for business in 1989. Good on you guys!

Author's Note: Spike is in the process of writing a semi autobiographical book which will be well worth looking out for (as is his novel centred around the Falklands War – *Cry Argentina*).

A Slow Windup

The presence of the ski lifts shifted the focus of most of the area's good skiers to Nevis Range's Back Corries where it became all too easy for the early instructors and patrollers to ski the usual suspects of Yellow Belly, Chancers, Easy Gully, Spikes and Summit Gully. The rush was on during that initial season to tick off all the obvious 'firsts', but how much of that involved steep skiing remains questionable.

One of the early avalanche forecasters, Mark Hughes, notched up a few notable descents during these formative years at Nevis Range including Yank's Gully (or The Funnel as it was known then) in Coire an Lochain with Andy Nelson in 1992, Bold Rush on the West Face with Graham Moss, followed by trips down Rush and Don't Rush circa 1994. Local kayaking legend Andy Jackson was also hot on the heels repeating Bold Rush with Mark soon after and then soloing Y Gully Left (to his girlfriend's dismay).

 skimountain

One of many kids to grow up skiing at Nevis Range during the early nineties

During the nineties a whole generation of local kids (including the author) grew up skiing at Nevis – hucking off cornices over the back was often the main aim, even if it meant being chased by then head of ski patrol Tony Cardwell – but very few if any 'different' routes got skied. It was June 1995 before the author, along with Neil Muir, skied on the Ben for the first time – hoping to ski the North Face but ending up descending the Red Burn in the clag instead (not for the first time!)

Around 1996 Nevis Range instructors Simon Christy and James Urquart showed willing by venturing further afield and ticked off a Triple Crown of Number 4 Gully, Carn Mor Dearg, and Chancers. And during the mid to late nineties interest in skiing the steep gullies on the Ben started to take hold again with a number of local skiers making trips up to repeat the more obvious routes such as Numbers 3, 4, 5, and Tower Gullies.

Number 2 Gully on the Ben was skied from below the cornice back in the eighties by Martin Burrows-Smith, but since has seen numerous groups from around the country thinking they were first to ski it from the top, with Gavin MacKay and Ben Thorburn in 1996, Al Reid and Ally Coul on telemarks in May 2001, and various groups from Fort William, Glencoe, Edinburgh, and elsewhere all making descents around this time.

Paul Raistrick took the Scottish mountain film festivals by storm with his two films *Pushing Winter*

(2003) and *The Old Rock* (2004). These films chronicled Paul snowboarding a variety of steep gullies around Scotland but especially on Ben Nevis – these films were all the more remarkable given the fact that he did the whole thing himself by fixing a camera on a tripod at the top, riding the line, then climbing back up to retrieve the camera. Douglas Brown, Matt McLaughlin, and Jamie Bartlett followed in the mid 2000's with more backcountry snowboarding films - *In Pursuit* and *Addicted to Snow* – featuring some great Back Corries, Carn Mor Dearg, and Ben Nevis boarding. Numerous other boarders have been riding steep lines in the area certainly since the early to mid nineties, with Number 4 Gully on the Ben being a particular favourite.

The carving ski revolution started to take hold during the early 2000's and the flood of new alpine ski touring bindings and modern touring boots with 'walk-modes' onto the scene from around 2005 onwards began to fuel a real revival of the ski touring and mountaineering mentality.

Mopping Up

By this time many of the most obvious lines on Aonach Mor and Ben Nevis had been skied but there was still a slow trickle of new descents being done, usually with very little fanfare during the pre-facebook era. Gavin MacKay skied Forgotten Twin in 2002 and then again in 2005; Steven Wilcox scraped his way down Raeburn's Easy Route in 2009 while John Sutherland, Kenny and Dave Biggin skied Spidery Walls during 2009 (on ice, with a boarder sliding over the cliffs the day after), and this was later repeated in 2010 by Gavin Caruthers down the chute in the middle with somewhat nicer snow. Liam Moynihan and Bob Hyde quietly took Hidden Gully by storm during 2010 (later repeated by the author and John Sutherland), and Peter MacKenzie and Al Todd ticked off Tower Ridge followed by Tower Gully for the Tower Double in 2013.

During 2013 and with the guidebook project already taking shape, the author finally got the bit between his teeth and notched up a good number of descents (some of which will have been skied previously) with a variety of others including Dave Biggin (White Russian & Vallee Verte), John Sutherland (Grotto Rush), Donald Paterson (3Rap Rush), and Neil Muir (The Bhealaich Face & Beag for Mor). This spree included all the West Face gullies of Aonach Mor, a couple more lines into the Back Corries, the East and West face gullies of Aonach Beag, several lines into An Cul Choire, along with repeats of a number of Ben Nevis gullies.

Exploration

No doubt lines have been skied on Ben Nevis and elsewhere in the area that have not made it into this guidebook. Apologies are offered to those whose exploits have been missed out – this section doesn't claim to be complete, only representative. Perhaps that is how it should be so that some 'first descents' always remain for those who seek them out. If you have info or wish to claim a line however, please share it so that it can be corrected and included in the next edition.

Technique

There isn't enough space here to go into a full run-down about how to ski or snowboard. However, there are a small number of common problems that creep into people's technique as soon as things steepen up so a few brief pointers are given to help with these below.

Skiing off the Cornice

This can be incredibly daunting for people, especially the first time. The best advice is of course to choose the right day, with the right people, and go to an easy entrance such as Winger Wall or Backtrack. You can often make the entrance much more forgiving with a little bit of pole whacking or even using a shovel or ice axe.

It's important to remember that (in most places) the slope will be at its steepest for the top ten metres or so – as soon as you get past that top steep section the slope usually eases off and you will find it much more forgiving. So don't try to stop yourself on the steepest section – instead, drop in on a slanting traverse aiming for a spot slightly further down and don't let things slide out of control but just aim to 'weather the storm' until you get there.

The steep section at the top almost always makes people do precisely the wrong thing – you try to hug the slope, perhaps even grabbing at it with your uphill hand. Instead, you must force yourself to dramatically over-emphasise the following:

- Look downhill.
- Get both arms and your shoulders pointing and stretching downhill – see if you can get your uphill hand and shoulders over your downhill ski.
- Get as much of your weight as possible going through your downhill ski.
- Lean forwards and let the skis slide until you are past the initial steep bit.

Steep Ground & Jump Turns

The angle of the slope actually needs to be very steep before you need to do jump turns. However, it's a skill well worth practising every time you're on a steep slope so that you have the skill in the bag for when you really need it.

Some good instruction will help you develop this skill and many others further, but having a look at the following sequence of photos should give you some idea of what you're aiming for.

photos **Kenny Biggin**
rider **John Sutherland**

Jump turn technique

Steep Control Turns

When the ground is very steep and you need to stay perfectly in control the best technique can be to start your turn much more slowly by planting your downhill pole and putting your uphill ski out in a bit of a wedge before lifting your downhill ski and sliding into the turn – the wedge with the uphill ski gives you a good platform to stand on and gets the turn started nice and securely before you leave the ground.

Steep Boarding Technique

In common with skiing, snowboarding on steep ground tends to make people do all the wrong things. On a snowboard you only have one edge so it is important to stand with your weight properly over it to give you the maximum chance of staying in control. As soon as you either sit down or lean onto the hill you are reducing the pressure being put through the edge and as such are more likely to loose grip. Most people have a preference as to whether they go in past cornices on their toe or heel edge – make sure your preference is for the right reasons (i.e. being able to sit down when you get scared on your heel edge, or hug the snow with your hands on your toe edge aren't good reasons!)

Just as important as maintaining pressure on your edge is being able to slide in control – many boarders go off the edge and slam the edge of the board sideways into the snow far too suddenly which often results in stopping too abruptly and being catapulted down the hill. Instead, get used to using a controlled slide to get you past the steep part before engaging the edge gradually. The more you practice side slipping and edge control on the pistes, the easier this will become when you really need it.

Sliding with Axes

Some people like to get their axe out when skiing or boarding something very steep – especially when edging their way past a steep cornice or scarp slope. The problem (and irony) with this is it changes the way you ski and board so in some ways may make you more likely to lose your edge, fall and need the axe. The technique should probably be saved for a very small set of situations.

Equipment

Having the right equipment makes a massive difference to your enjoyment of the sport. It's well worth taking some time to research what bits of kit are right for you, asking around for advice if you're not sure, and if something isn't working for you don't be afraid to change it – this is the ebay generation after all! The advice below was correct at the time of writing (2013) but of course equipment changes over time so if you are reading this in 2030 be aware that things have moved on!

Skis

Choice of ski will depend hugely on how you want to ski and what your priorities are. In general for offpiste skiing in Scotland you will want an 'All Mountain', 'Park & Pipe', 'Freeride' or 'Touring' ski between 85 and 100mm underfoot – there is never really enough powder here to require a fatter 'Big Mountain' ski unless you really plan to go big! At the narrower end of this range the skis will be better on piste and ice, but will struggle to float on powder or drive through crud.

Kit for a day on Ben Nevis – skis + touring bindings, ice axes, light crampons, GPS, map, compass, whistle, food + water, first aid + head torch + bivvy bag, skins + harscheisen, transceiver, shovel + probe, mobile, warm clothes + helmet

Appropriate ski length varies with the type of ski but also with your height, weight, and ability – for a good skier of an average weight looking for a 95cm freeride ski, a good place to start is a ski that's about the same height as you. If you are heavy for your height or very strong, good, or aggressive, you could go slightly (5cm) longer – likewise if you are light, still learning, or fairly cautious, you could go around 10cm shorter than your height. In general narrower skis with shorter turn radii should be shorter than fatter, wide turn radius skis.

The ski's radius is another important thing to think about – this dictates how tightly the ski will naturally turn. For instance a turn radius of 13metres will 'want' to do rapid short and tight turns (good on narrow pistes!), while a ski with a 20metre or longer radius will want to go quite fast and straight with great big long wide turns being its forte. In general, the better you get the more able to cope with a longer turn radius you will be. Around 17metres is quite a good radius for an average offpiste ski as it will happily do short controlled turns on piste, but still be stable enough to open up into long GS type turns when a powder bowl opens out in front of you. If all you want to do is huck off the cornice and straight line things, then a big radius will suit you fine (though it may not do your on-piste technique many favours!)

If you choose a pair of 'Touring' skis they are likely to be much lighter weight than conventional skis – that is great for hiking and skinning up things, though note their skiing performance (and therefore your technique) will often suffer as a result so as always you need to weigh up the compromises.

Ski Bindings

For general skiing around most modern alpine ski bindings will be fine – just make sure the DIN settings go up high enough to suit your size and your style of skiing.

If you plan to skin uphill anywhere you will want to consider a pair of touring bindings. There are a number of options to choose from – in essence they split into two types: Pin bindings and Step-in.

Step-in touring bindings allow you to use either normal alpine ski boots or touring boots. They are generally significantly heavier than pin bindings but many skiers prefer them as they are much closer to conventional alpine bindings in terms of how they look and work. There are many beefy options for this type of binding and although these are heavy for skinning uphill, they are more than capable of going hard and even hucking off drops, etc.

Pin bindings popular on the continent are rising in popularity in Britain although they still seem very alien to many. You can only use them with touring boots that have in-built metal inserts at the toe and heel. They are significantly lighter weight than the step-in alternatives so are becoming the option of choice for anyone serious about touring or ski mountaineering. They do have a DIN release and in recent years there have been some models with higher DIN's (12 and even higher) coming on the scene aimed at people who want to ski hard. Some of the lighter pin binding models are super-minimalist and don't even have brakes fitted, which will be acceptable for some die-hard tourers but perhaps a step too far for more casual offpiste skiers.

Often the decision between step-in or pin bindings comes down to whether you are ready to change to touring boots with integrated pin inserts or not, and whether your priorities are keeping the weight down or maximising robustness.

Ski Boots

By far the best boots to help you learn to ski well are normal stiff alpine ski boots. Far too many people start skiing in floppy touring boots before they've had a chance to develop their technique – this may be a comfy option but ultimately limits your progression. The best advice is to learn to ski with good technique on and off piste using stiff alpine boots, then get a pair of stiff touring boots as a second pair once you have learnt to ski well. Whenever the conditions aren't great offpiste, get your stiff alpine boots out and go and work on your technique using the lifts.

Normal ski boots are great if all you want to do is use the lifts or do an occasional 20 minute boot pack up to the top of a head-wall, or traverse that bit further over to get to the untracked stuff, but if you want to do any serious hiking or skinning to get your dream lines then normal ski boots start to become a less-than-ideal tool for the job.

Normal downhill ski boots have a number of shortcomings in the backcountry:

- They're super-stiff and have a constant fixed forward lean (good for skiing but rubbish for walking or skinning in).
- They have a smooth, flat sole designed for alpine DIN bindings (which aren't great when it comes to hiking over rocks or icy stuff).
- They're heavy - fine for sliding but it soon adds up when you keep having to lift one foot above the other!)
- They tend to be tight - great for cranking on piste, but try kicking steps or trudging for any length of time and you'll lose toenails!

The Alternatives - Ski Touring Boots

There are a number of alternatives, all of which fall into the fairly broad category of 'Alpine Ski Touring Boots'.

In general heavier boots are better for going downhill and the lighter ones are better for going up. At the heavy end of the scale there are some conventional downhill boots with an added walk mode – these are OK for short hikes and skins but not great for anything longer. Then there are a selection of stiff touring boots that still have four buckles and a high flex rating but also have a proper rockered vibram sole with a good walk mode – these are probably the category best suited for the majority of skiing in this book as they can perform quite well as downhill boots while still being slightly lighter and much more comfortable for long uphills. As you go lighter than this the boots generally become

more suited for outings such as hut-to-hut tours in the Alps where a lot of the focus is about the journey rather than the difficulty of the skiing. Ski touring boots aimed at hut-to-hut tours are often not stiff or tall enough (i.e. they don't come as high up your shin) to be able to ski really hard or technically well in.

Telemark Kit

Telemarking still remains a minority sport which probably is part of the attraction for some. Freeing the heel often provides a new challenge for good skiers and there's no doubt that there is something inherently cool about seeing someone ripping down a slope doing tele turns (especially if she is Scandinavian and blonde)! Specific telemark ski designs are available with varying flex patterns, but the majority of telemarkers use whichever conventional alpine ski they like the look of.

There are two main boot and binding types to choose from – 75mm cable bindings or NTN. There is also the traditional 3 pin binding system which is the lightest option and favoured for some touring setups, but doesn't provide the same level of control for downhill use so these are fairly old fashioned now for most freeskiing purposes.

Cable bindings are still the most common and work with boots with a 75mm 'duckbill' at the toe. As cable bindings and boots have become more stiff and powerful they have also ironically got less suitable for touring uphill because the springs tend to make the ski tips dive. Some cable bindings have a touring mode which removes the resistance when going uphill. Most cable bindings don't come off when you fall, although there are a few bindings which do offer a release function.

The newcomer on the block is the Rottefella NTN system which instead of cables and duckbills uses boots with an extra ledge under your foot that gets clamped into the toepiece. NTN stands for New Telemark Norm and was designed to solve some of the long standing problems with cable bindings.

NTN bindings are step-in, provide resistance-free touring modes, and also have a release mechanism to save your legs if you fall. They also have the added advantage that you can jump straight into an alpine touring binding should the need arise, and some boots also have Dynafit inserts.

Both NTN and cable bindings are good options for telemarkers and which you choose will be down to your priorities and personal preference.

photo Reamonn Leakas | riders Dougie Pryce, Ryan Thompson, G... ...Lellan

Split Boards & Snowshoes

For snowboarders wanting to access terrain requiring lengthy uphills there are two main choices – either a split board or snowshoes (though many boarders make do without either). Split boards have got a lot better in the last few years and let boarders divide the board in two, flip the bindings round, and then skin uphill in the same way as skiers. You can either buy a split board new or buy a kit to convert an

photo Ron ...
rider Andy Burton
A split board in touring mode

existing board – which you choose will depend on budget, DIY skills, and whether you already have a board that you really want to use in the backcountry. There are also adapter kits out there that let you use lightweight Dynafit bindings on your split board. Check out Voile and SparkR&D kit for starters.

The (usually cheaper) alternative to split boards is snowshoes – these are fairly lightweight and can easily be carried on the front of your pack. Whether you go for a split board or snowshoes, you will also want to get a pair of collapsible poles which can also come in handy on long traverses.

photo **Ron Cameron** | rider **Andy Burton**

A split board in riding mode (Beinn Teallach)

Snowboard Boots

The majority of snowboarders ride in soft boots but these start to have limitations if you plan on doing significant amounts of touring or ski mountaineering. Although soft boots can be used with both snowshoes and crampons (using strap models), hard shell or ski touring boots are generally much better suited to coping with clambering around in steep terrain – they are far more capable of kicking steps on steeper snowslopes and have the toe bails and stiffness needed for use with step in crampons. As with most things, there are compromises to be made and at the end of the day it will depend on your preferences and priorities as to the type of boots that work for you.

Skins & Ski Crampons

Some of the routes in this book are best accessed using skins which stick to the bottom of your skis or split board and allow you to go uphill. Try to get skins that are a mix of mohair and synthetic fibres so that you get good durability and waterproofing while still getting a good bit of glide. Try also to make sure your skins fit your skis well – the skin should cover as much of the base material as possible but leave the metal edges exposed the whole way along. Having skins with solid attachments at the tip and tail is also important – if they keep pinging off you should change the attachment to something more secure.

For skinning on crust and ice on steeper slopes you need ski crampons (called harscheisen in German or couteaux in French) – these are specific to your touring bindings and are well worth carrying for the amount of difference they make to being able to skin up something when conditions get tough.

Mountaineering Equipment

As you start to ski or board steeper and more adventurous routes you need to be prepared to use some basic mountaineering techniques. Initially, this may just involve taking an ice axe and crampons which will help get you out of trouble if you need to retreat back up a gully, or enable you to get past a steeper pitch if you're having trouble skinning up.

You can get some very lightweight step-in crampons which are perfect - easy to carry and more than capable of coping with the sort of ground you're likely to encounter. There are also some very lightweight axes available but note that some of these are not very suitable for use clambering up steep ground, particularly if you are more of a skier than a climber and need something solid to pound into the snow to give you confidence – you need to find the right compromise between weight and function. If you are planning to climb up any of the steeper gullies prior to skiing them you may well find it easier with two axes instead of one, especially if you are new to mountaineering.

For anyone intending to either rope in to assess snow conditions or determined to access tricky gully entrances, you may want to carry a rope. In this area a thin (8mm) 30metre rope is about right – get a 'twin' or 'glacier' rope with 'dry' or 'super dry' treatment. Ideal is if one of your buddies has a similar rope so that you can abseil the full 30metres if required and then retrieve the ropes. To go with the

photo Kenny Biggin | rider Donald Paterson

Setting up anchors on the first rap of Don't Rush

rope you will also need a lightweight harness, a belay / abseil device (make sure it provides enough friction with the thin rope), and probably a selection of crabs, slings, and a prussik or two.

A small selection of the routes in this book require abseils to get past short ice pitches or rocky patches. For these routes you will need to be more prepared – note that unlike in some places in the Alps, there are no in-situ bolts to use so any abseiling will be done using anchors you set up yourself. Consider a small selection of nuts, extra slings or 'tat' and even pitons or Abalakov kit (long ice screw, threader tool and cord).

Cutting a snow bollard to check conditions

Carrying just the right kit on any particular day is an art - your skiing technique and speed uphill will suffer dramatically if your rucksack is too big. So choose wisely, try to plan ahead, and embrace a safe but minimalist attitude.

On the second abseil pitch of Don't Rush

photo **Kenny Biggin** | rider **Donald Paterson**

The author exploring the West Face – near the top of Grotto Rush

About The Author

After learning to ski in the West Highland Ski Club at Glencoe in the late eighties, Kenny Biggin grew up skiing the Back Corries of Nevis Range and has skied there for at least part of most seasons since it first opened almost 25 years ago. Back in the day he was an instructor at Nevis Range with forays to the Alps instructing in Italy during the mid-90s. In 2007 Kenny founded the SkiMountain brand as a way to build his life around his passion for skiing. Latterly, he has been seeking out steeper and deeper slopes worldwide and has skied and toured in the backcountry of New Zealand, Canada, Norway, and of course the Alps. However, he still considers Fort William home (although the Alps comes a close second during the season!)

Kenny rarely skis a day at Nevis Range without going 'over the back' or further afield in a massive variety of conditions and reckons he has skied the Back Corries hundreds if not thousands of times.

△ skimountain

Thanks for the Support

Snowgoose Mountain Centre & Calluna Self Catering